AMHERST
FROM TAVERNS TO A TOWN

Robert C. Wimer

Leah Settle Gibbs

With contributing authors
Patty Walton Turpin
Thurman B. Davis
James D. Settle
and others

BLACKWELL
PRESS
LYNCHBURG, VIRGINIA

Cover:
The west side of Main Street, Amherst, has been the heart of the town for more than a century. Starting on back cover, from left, are Wade Wood's store, Kent's store, Hatcher's drug store, Post Office, and Andrew Watts' store, shown in the late 1920s.
Amherst County Historical Museum photo

Title page:
Building that served as Amherst Post Office until 1923, at the corner of Main and Second streets.
Paul Wailes III photo

Contents page:
John L. "Jack" Lee built this house at 327 South Main Street in 1885 while serving as commonwealth's attorney for Amherst County. The structure later became the home of former clerk of Amherst County Circuit Court, William E. Sandidge Jr. His son, Richard, lives there today.
Elizabeth A. Langhorne photo

© 2010 by Hunting Tower, LLC

All rights reserved. Published 2010

First edition

ISBN: 978-0-9779523-9-7

Library of Congress Control Number: 2010914790

Printed in the United States of America

Published by Blackwell Press, Lynchburg, Virginia

BLACKWELL
PRESS

Contact Blackwell Press at:
311 Rivermont Avenue
Lynchburg, Virginia 24504
434-528-4665
Email:Sales@BlackwellPress.net
www.BlackwellPress.net

CONTENTS

Emma and Virgil Bernard and two of their children walk along South Main Street.
Paul Wailes III photo

West side of Main Street around 1950
The News & Advance photo

Rexall DRUGS

AMHERST ELECTRIC CO.

DRUMMONDS

Aerial photo of Amherst in the 1930s. Notice construction of Route 60 in upper left. Courthouse is just left of center.
Florence Nixon photo

PREFACE

When Leah Settle Gibbs gathered us together for lunch near the end of May 2009, we were dubious. Another committee, more meetings. But we listened. She was proposing at least twenty-six stories relating to the history of the Town of Amherst to be printed in the *Amherst New Era-Progress*, the town's weekly newspaper.

That would be a story every two weeks throughout the town's Centennial Year—2010. Were we up to it? Could we produce that many stories? And could we meet that deadline—a story every two weeks?

The task seemed daunting, but we were all willing to give it a try. It was a good project, we decided, and certainly worth pursuing in terms of recording a bit of the town's history over its first 100 years.

The next thing we needed was a list of story ideas—at least twenty-six stories. Probably more than that since it was inevitable that some stories would not pan out. So, we put together the list and assigned the writers who were interested in taking on the subject.

Recognizing that some stories would be more difficult than others, we decided it would be prudent to get at least half the stories finished before we even began the series. That would give us some time to fall back on in the event that a story fell through.

It was a fascinating process. As the five of us met during the fall, we shared the results of interviews with various folks around town who were tuned in to the town's history, not the least of whom was Paul Wailes III. It turned out, as is noted elsewhere in the book, that whenever we couldn't find the answer to a question, we would turn to Paul. We are indebted to many others who took the time to share reminiscences and photos with us.

We discovered a number of stories that we had never heard; we uncovered tidbits that we decided had to be in the stories, but we didn't know which ones at the time. The Judge Campbell story, for example, was new to us, although parts of it had been printed before. It was exciting to hear new details or see old photos that reflected life in the town eighty to 100 years ago.

One of the threads running through the book focuses on the interesting people who have added to the town's history. Some people are called "town characters," others are called "institutions." But all have high visibility and a quality that has allowed them to be remembered years later. That's what makes a small town unique.

Where else could one be recognized at a distance by his profile, his gait, his shape, his hat, his daily routine, his greeting, his car or even the car's speed (or lack thereof), or perhaps the way that car is parked? Some folks are remembered because they emptied trash cans, others because they enforced the law, and others simply because they were there, every day, on a predictable schedule. Vignettes of a few of Amherst's memorable people are included within these pages.

As the first stories were printed in the newspaper, thanks to the efforts of Scott Marshall, managing editor, we found they were generating lots of interest among readers in town. By summer of the Centennial Year, we had more than 26 stories, mostly as a result of one story leading us to another or some stories that were too long and had to be broken into two parts to accommodate the newspaper's space limitations.

About the same time, we all reported talking to folks around town who said they hoped we were saving the stories and that maybe we could gather them together in a book. We liked the idea, especially because a book would give us more space for photos that were left out of the newspaper stories and more space for the stories themselves.

Amherst: From Taverns to a Town is the result of more than a year's work of compiling information, gathering photographs from dozens of sources and putting it together in what we believe is an interesting story about the history of the town. We hope you enjoy it.

—The authors
Sept. 30, 2010

THE CENTENNIAL YEAR

The year 2010 marked the centennial of the incorporation of the Town of Amherst. Various commemorations of that event were held throughout the year. This series of stories reflecting the town's rich and colorful history is one of them.

Among the suggestions for the centennial observance was that a compilation of Amherst history be produced in an enduring format. Toward that end, a group representing numerous years and generations of local history was assembled. This series of reminiscences of the way Amherst and its people lived in the century following 1910 was launched as a yearlong bi-weekly feature in the *Amherst New Era-Progress*. Committee members interviewed a sizable contingent of current and former Amherst citizens. Sources also included newspapers and books on local history as well as other written accounts, such as information gleaned from the proceedings of town business.

The series of stories that follows begins with some notes on the early days of Amherst County and "the village," and proceeds through accounts of daily life, the memorable people, and even animals, from around town. The accounts also include schools and businesses, generational forms of entertainment and social diversions, with some emphasis on the impact of larger events such as World War II and the transition from a primarily rural economy.

The following committee members have researched and developed materials for these articles. Brief biographies of the committee members follow:

Thurman B. Davis moved with his family to Amherst as a 14-year-old in 1957 when his father became pastor of Amherst Baptist Church. He has been an Amherst County resident since that time, and is now retired from teaching history in the Lynchburg city school system. He inherited his father's interest in the people and history of the area; the Rev. Bailey Davis published a number of books and articles on genealogy. Thurman Davis' wife, Mary Gayle, is a native of Amherst County whose family has a long history in the area.

Courtesy of
Stephen LeBar

Pulpwood Festival parade in 1956,
at Main and Second Street.
Amherst New Era-Progress photo

Leah Settle Gibbs is a lifelong resident of Amherst County. She taught in the Amherst County school system from 1970 until 1988. Her parents' families were from Central Virginia, both having moved to the town around 1910 after living in the rural areas of Amherst and Nelson counties. Her husband, Phil, who is deceased, was a physician in Lynchburg from 1965 until his retirement in 1999.

James D. Settle, "Jimmy" or "Jim," spent his pre-college life in Amherst. After careers in both government service and private, non-profit social service, he retired a few years ago with his wife, Kay, also a Central Virginian and amateur genealogist, to the suburbs of Lynchburg. History has long been one of his principal avocations and delights. He, along with his sister, Leah, comprised the audience for many family stories and local history recollections which accompanied the Sunday drives with kinfolk through the countryside and local cemeteries.

Patty Ann Walton Turpin came as a two-year-old with her family to her mother's hometown, and is now retired from teaching in the Nelson County school system. Her youth was spent in a multi-generational home within a stone's throw of the Amherst traffic circle; she possesses long lines of Amherst roots, including her grandfather, Dr. R. B. Ware, the consummate country doctor. She and her husband, Ralph, an attorney, reside in Lovingston.

Robert C. "Bob" Wimer, moved to Amherst in 1950 as a seven-year-old. His mother, Elizabeth, was managing editor for the *Amherst New Era-Progress* and served many years on the school board. Having lived here continuously since 1971, he has deep Amherst connections. Wimer worked briefly for the *Amherst New Era-Progress* and is now retired from the position of editorial page editor of *The News & Advance* in Lynchburg. His wife, Betty, is also an Amherst native and retired English and Latin teacher.

Many of the accounts in this book, it should be emphasized, are based on personal recollections. Sources have been cited throughout the stories, but it should be noted from the outset that the authors must register a significant debt of gratitude to "The Encyclopedia of Amherst," Paul Wailes III, eighty-one-year-old native son, whose maternal ancestors had been in the area in the early days of Amherst County, and whose grandfather Wailes came to Amherst in 1903 from the Rockfish Valley of Nelson County. Wailes possesses a virtually flawless memory of the details of life in the community and an inexhaustible fund of stories—amusing, sad, or instructive—about its people and their history. His ability to recall names, dates, places, and events is nothing short of staggering.

As committee members met and compared notes and findings, numerous questions arose. It soon became apparent that every question had one of two possible answers: (1) the actual answer that someone had already discovered; or (2) "I don't know, but you can ask Paul Wailes."

The committee in no way presumes to be the authority on the history of all families, places, organizations, businesses, and events in the town of Amherst. All individuals have their own perspectives on the circumstances of their lives.

Front: Bob Wimer, Leah Gibbs; Second row: Patty Turpin, Thurman Davis, Jim Settle.
Virginia Sykora photo

Another day of business in Amherst takes shape in 1910 as these men gather in front of the Bank of Amherst.
From left are Bev Harrison, Houston Joyner, Ed Bowman, Stickley Tucker, unidentified, and Kinckle Allen.
This building was renovated in the 1940s by Robert Bethel, who then opened a jewelry and clock shop.
Amherst County Historical Museum photo

ACKNOWLEDGMENTS

It would be nearly impossible to come up with all the names of those who helped make this book a reality. We had to ask about residents who would know certain details we thought were important to this history of the Town of Amherst. Once we discovered their names, those folks were unfailing in their efforts to help us recall the past of our little town.

Paul Wailes III, of course, was instrumental in guiding us in the right direction and inspiring us in the search for what we deemed was important to the history of the town's beginnings.

Lots of other people helped us along the way. They included, but are no means limited to, Ben Smith, Helen Massie, Peggy Gregory Lau, Harold Higgins, Jean Higginbotham, Tommy Littrell, Dickie and Virginia Wydner, Jackie Williams Beidler, Lloyd Dearborn Wells, Will and Susan Mays, Page and Mary B. Stinnett, Dorothy Kent Harvey, and Jackie Ware.

Our thanks are also extended to H. L. Hansberry, Lynn Kable, Jean Higginbotham, and Jack Hobbs for their contributions.

Many of the photographs in this book came from Paul Wailes' vast collection from the town's early years. Others came from the collection of the Amherst County Historical Museum and newspapers, including The *Amherst New Era-Progress* and *The News & Advance* in Lynchburg.

We have attempted to research and credit the photographer and the owners of the photographs and other images whenever possible. Many, we believe, are in the public domain, but we are sure there are still a few that we have neglected to properly credit. For that, we apologize in advance and hope that the benefit of getting the information in the hands of the public will outweigh unintended errors.

We are also indebted to Nancy Blackwell Marion, a daughter of Amherst County, whose judgment in selecting old photographs is outstanding. Her ability to select photos that capture the time and the mood of years gone by is virtually without parallel.

To all who helped with this history of the Town of Amherst, we thank you.

—Robert C. Wimer
—Leah Settle Gibbs

Early Years

Main Street, Amherst,
looking south toward the
Central Hotel, around 1912.
Nancy Marion photo

The brick courthouse replaced a wooden structure in 1870. Additions were made at the rear of the building in 1935, with further additions in 1961. A major expansion and renovation was completed in 1998.
Amherst County Historical Museum photo

LORD JEFFERY AMHERST

By Robert C. Wimer

Historians who search for a connection between the town of Amherst and its namesake, Lord Jeffery Amherst, will continue to be disappointed. The Lord of Amherst, as he came to be known, never set foot in the Virginia colony, let alone the town that bears his name in Central Virginia.

Amherst is best known as one of the victors in the French and Indian War (1754 to 1763). He was commanding general of the British forces during the final battles of the war, winning victories against the French to acquire Canada for England. In the process, he helped make England the world's chief colonizer at the conclusion of the Seven Years War among the colonial powers in Europe.

The town of Amherst, Mass., was named for the general, whose adventures in North America did take him there. Amherst College was later named after the town. At the time of the naming of the Massachusetts town, according to one historian, Jeffery Amherst was "the most glamorous military hero in the New World."

Numerous other places in the United States and Canada are also named for him including cities and towns in Ohio, New Hampshire, New York, Nebraska, Texas, Colorado, South Dakota, Wisconsin, and Nova Scotia.

Amherst was born at Riverhead, Kent, England, and was first commissioned as an ensign in the foot guards in 1731. During the Seven Years War in Europe, he was selected from relative obscurity to lead the British assault on Louisbourg, Nova Scotia (1758), the first in a series of victorious battles that would give England supremacy over the French in Canada. As commander-in-chief in North America, he played a direct role in occupying former French positions at Fort Ticonderoga in upstate New York. He completed his triumph with the capture of Montreal in 1760.

A year later, 1761, in a totally unrelated event, Amherst County was formed from parts of Albemarle and named for Jeffery Amherst, undoubtedly because of the acclaim he had received with his victories in Canada. Although there are several spellings for his first name, Amherst himself spelled his name Jeffery.

Incidentally, the town's original name was

The Lord of Amherst

Five Oaks. When Nelson County was formed from the northern half of Amherst County in 1807, the county seat was moved from Cabellsville (now Colleen) to the village of Five Oaks, which was later changed to Amherst, probably in deference to the name of the county.

As a reward for his military success, Amherst was appointed governor-general of British North America, a position he held until 1763. Later that same year, Amherst was appointed the colonial governor of Virginia, a position that provided compensation despite his not being called upon to make any decisions. In fact, the record shows he never came to Virginia. Later in 1763, Amherst returned home to England and was subsequently removed as Governor of Virginia for refusing to return to the colony and govern in person.

Despite his fame, Amherst's name became tarnished by stories of smallpox-infected blankets used as germ warfare against American Indians. It was an early example—perhaps the first—of biological warfare. Although the record clearly shows that Amherst detested the Indians he had to fight on his way to victory in Canada and later, historians have debated just how personally he became involved in the germ warfare.

Letters and other documents exchanged between General Amherst and his officers and others during the summer of 1763 shed more light on the subject. The British were fighting what became known as Pontiac's Rebellion after Pontiac, an Ottawa chief who had sided with the French, led an uprising against the British after the French surrender in Canada.

One of Amherst's officers suggested in a letter dated July 13, 1763, distribution of blankets to "inoculate the Indians." In a return letter, Amherst approved the plan and suggested

Lord Jeffery Amherst was never actually in the town and county that bear his name.

further "every other method that can serve to Extirpate this Execrable Race." Another letter from Amherst to his officer directly raised the question this way: "Could it not be contrived to send the Small Pox among those disaffected tribes of Indians? We must on this occasion use every stratagem in our power to reduce them."

Another writer, R. G. Robertson, indicts Amherst this way in his 2001 book with the quaint title of "Rotting Face: Smallpox and the American Indian." After describing Amherst as "an arrogant aristocrat who despised all Indians," he points out that "Amherst withheld gunpowder and lead from France's former native allies, stating that England's enemies ought to be punished, not rewarded. When informed that the tribes depended on their muskets for taking game and would starve without ammunition, he remained unswayed, callously informing his aides that they should seed the complaining bands with smallpox so as to lend starvation a speedy hand."

That's not a pretty image of the man for whom the town gains its name.

Where did this military hero's allegiance fall during the Revolutionary War that began in 1775? Historians report that because of his close ties with many Americans, he refused to take a field command during the war. He did, however, serve in an advisory role for the British cause, probably from a base in England.

Amherst became a baron in 1776 and a field marshal in 1778. Baron Amherst of Montreal, as he came to be known in his last years, died on his country estate, Sevenoaks, England, in 1797 at the age of 80. It has been written that he was much honored by his fellow countrymen.

The town of Amherst, Va., is testimony to the endurance of a military hero who governed the state in name only, but who never graced the town or its environs with his commanding presence. ∞

JUDGE CAMPBELL
AND THE ANTI-SALOON LEAGUE

By Robert C. Wimer

One hundred years ago, on April 15, 1910, the village of Amherst became an incorporated town, a change that gave residents the opportunity to create and enforce local ordinances and generate the revenue needed to fund local projects. The first order of business on the new town's agenda entailed instituting fines for concealed weapons and public drunkenness. As the county seat, the small village of Amherst had endured more than its fair share of traffic, transients, taverns, prostitutes, and alcohol-fueled brawls. Even the courthouse steps were not safe by any standards imaginable today. By incorporating, villagers hoped to get a better handle on the situation.

Recalling stories he heard from his elders in the 1930s, Paul Wailes III, the town's unofficial historian, explains that the village and its surroundings had a drinking problem. As many as fifteen saloons dotted the streets and alleys from the railroad station up Depot Street and into the upper village.

It is likely that one of those taverns was located in the Central Hotel, which was razed in

1953 to make way for the shopping center that contained Drummond's grocery store, Wailes' clothing shop, and Howell's grocery. Older town residents can still remember buying coffee and pickled eggs at the hotel's coffee shop before it was torn down.

In the early days those who patronized the saloons, which were also variously referred to as barrooms and taverns, were given to lawlessness on occasion. That lawlessness, says Wailes, reached a point after the turn of the century that "the wives of all the attorneys accompanied their husbands to court for fear of what might happen. And they [the husbands] were armed."

Villagers did have a voice. Local option laws allowed Virginia's magisterial districts to put questions of local concern on their ballots from election to election. Depending on which way the political winds were blowing, the volatile issue of banning or permitting the sale of alcohol would be put to a vote this way. In the years leading up to statewide prohibition (Virginia

Cadet Clarence J. Campbell at VMI. Virginia Military Institute archives photo

went "dry" in 1916; a few years later the rest of the nation followed suit), Amherst County citizens elected to ban the sale of all spirits except medicinal alcohol during one late nineteenth-century campaign, only to reverse their decision in a subsequent election.

Throughout the "wet" versus "dry" debate, temperance advocates tended to make strides, trip up, and then regain their footing. And, while many local leaders voted "dry," they themselves had no problem with alcohol and imbibed on a regular basis.

The Campbells Are Coming!

The road to the incorporation of the village of Amherst was filled with bumps. One of them was Amherst trial Judge Clarence J. Campbell and his encounter with a representative of the Virginia Anti-Saloon League. It was a case that generated widespread attention in the state's newspapers and drew some national coverage for the little village of Amherst. The coverage, however, did not always reflect favorably on the village or its people.

Although the county had voted to go dry in terms of the sale and manufacture of alcohol in 1898, according to authors C. C. Pearson and J. Edwin Hendricks in their book, *Liquor and Anti-Liquor in Virginia, 1619-1919*, at least one of the barrooms became a drug store.

In 1901, the drug store operated by S. A. Day dispensed as many as thirty barrels of "medicated whiskey" without violating the law in the opinion of the county judge. Al-

though charges were brought against the druggist under the local option laws in effect at the time, the judge, Clarence J. Campbell, instructed the jury to make decisions within a framework that could lead to only one conclusion: they had to find Mr. Day innocent.

A year later, the Rev. Charles H. Crawford, a Baptist preacher and superintendent of the Virginia Anti-Saloon League, got word of the court case and made an issue of it in his Anti-Saloon League newspaper, *The Christian Federation*. Crawford wrote of the judge's ruling in his newspaper that it wasn't clear which was doctored more—the whiskey or the judge.

Judge Campbell didn't take the criticism lightly. In response, he had the clergyman arraigned for contempt of court. When he failed to get a conviction on the contempt charge, the judge publicly horsewhipped the reverend on the Amherst courthouse steps. As *The New York Times* described it in a story on June 25, 1902, the whipping took place in the "presence of many ladies" and came "without warning." The paper reported that the judge struck the minister "several blows about the face and head, inflicting painful wounds." The *Washington Post* carried a similar account of the story.

The judge, according to the *Times'* story, had held that the accused druggist was merely selling whiskey for medicines allowed under the law. The sensational headline over the story was "Judge Cowhides Minister." That, surely, impressed the *Times'* readers with life below the Mason-Dixon Line.

The story went on to point out that Judge Campbell, an 1884 graduate of Virginia Military Institute, was the Amherst representative to the 1901 state Constitutional Convention and a prominent politician in Amherst County.

Campbell also represented Amherst in the House of Delegates from 1891 to 1898, when he resigned to accept Gov. Charles T. O'Ferral's appointment to the bench.

THE TIMES–DISPATCH. RICHMOND, VA., TUESDAY, FEBRUARY 10, 1903.

"THE CAMPBELLS ARE COMING!"

CAMPBELL CASE TO BE RESUMED TO=DAY

The public whipping in Amherst catapulted the Anti-Saloon League of Virginia into national prominence and led to the removal of Judge Campbell from the bench by the General Assembly in May 1903. The judge's appeal to the Supreme Court of Virginia was not successful.

A court-like investigation by the House of Delegates Courts of Justice Committee in February 1902 into the question of whether he should be removed from the bench provoked intense interest throughout the state. The *Richmond Times-Dispatch* covered it from start to finish, referring to the legal proceeding on several occasions as "sensational and remarkable."

On the first day of the newspaper's coverage, a cartoon accompanied the story depicting a number of half-man half-camel creatures on a long road from the little courthouse in the hills of Amherst to the majestic state Capitol in Richmond. Many of the man-camels carried jugs strapped over their humps—jugs that presumably were filled with whiskey. The caption on the cartoon read: "The Campbells Are Coming!"

The sensational part of the proceeding, of course, was the judge who had whipped the minister with his leather horsewhip, or cowhide as they called it in those days. Judge Campbell, who was thirty-nine years old at the time of the hearing, even brought the cowhide to the hearing room to describe how he used it and why. He testified that when he encountered Crawford outside the courtroom in Amherst, he gave him a chance to apologize for the unkind remarks he had made about the judge in his newspaper. The clergyman refused, saying, "I have made my statement."

At that point, Campbell said he raised his arm "and with this little whip struck him over the head. He dodged and I struck again."

Testimony during the hearing indicated that it was a common practice in Amherst to borrow prescription bottles and get them filled at Day's drug store —a pharmacy that only months before had been a barroom.

JUDGE CAMPBELL ILLUSTRATES THE WHIPPING.

Judge Campbell demonstrates horsewhip to the House of Delegates Courts of Justice Committee
From *Richmond Times-Dispatch*, Courtesy of Library of Virginia

Day, described as a "star witness" in the news accounts, testified that before he became a druggist, which was also before the local option laws went into effect, he sold whiskey in a regularly licensed saloon in Amherst. It just happened to become a drug store after the Courthouse District voted to ban the sale of whiskey.

Following the horsewhipping administered by Campbell, a grand jury indicted him on charges of felonious assault. The judge was acquitted in the subsequent jury trial, amid charges that whiskey somehow made its way into the jury room. It was further alleged that Judge Campbell had a hand in that, but he denied it throughout the legislative hearings.

During that jury trial, as reported in an Amherst County Museum newsletter story, Judge Campbell's assault on the Rev. Crawford could not be denied. But the "defense argued and won on a basis that gave Campbell the right to beat a 'Yankee parson' for insulting a Virginian."

While Judge Campbell's removal from the bench ended his judicial career, it didn't hurt him politically, it seems. By 1922, the people of Amherst elected him once again to the House of Delegates where he was assigned to the Courts of Justice Committee, the same committee that had recommended his removal from the bench nineteen years earlier.

After Judge Campbell was removed from the

View looking west from Amherst Courthouse, around 1928, showing the barrier gate erected to keep livestock off the Courthouse Green.
Paul Wailes III photo

bench in Amherst, the local temperance movement began gathering a full head of steam—perhaps because the barrooms were back in business. On the eve of the village's incorporation as a town in 1910, the town fathers were ready to wield their new authority to restore law and order to the streets of the little village that was the county seat of Amherst. ∽

THE VOORHEES WOMEN

Anne King and
Rebecca Voorhees
Paul Wailes III photo

As Rebecca Voorhees, late in life, lay in her bed telling stories of a century of life in Amherst, a youthful Paul Wailes III sat near the foot, listened and remembered. Mrs. Voorhees, daughter of Dr. John Thompson, recalled having heard the guns from Appomattox in 1865. Mrs. Voorhees met her husband, a Civil War veteran from Tennessee, when he came to Amherst to practice medicine with her father.

Mrs. Voorhees' nurse and aide, Anne King, who was born near "The Canebrakes" in western Amherst County during slavery years, remained in the Voorhees household until her death in 1927.

Rebecca's daughter, Margaret Voorhees, remained at home to attend her mother in her declining years. She herself developed as a "town character" in her own right, with many memorable quotations:

"I'm rejoicing today because I was never able to catch a man."

"Amherst is an easy place to lose your reputation, but a good place to live without one."

"Every woman ought to be able to have one baby with no questions asked."

"I always look forward to going to church: I sing a little, I look a little, and I pray a little."

After her brother's death as a young adult, Miss Margaret wrote him a letter every day, then "mailed" it to an old trunk. Her instructions after her death required the burning of these letters—hence, a day-to-day history of Amherst, covering a half-century, went up in smoke.

TOWN'S INCORPORATION
TRACED TO UNRULY SALOONS

By Robert C. Wimer

Life in Amherst at the time the town incorporated was not easy. Recollections of everyday affairs, nevertheless, offer a picture of hard work that made lives for the 650 or so residents as comfortable as possible.

The lack of basic amenities may indicate otherwise. There was no running water or electricity. Several trips daily to a nearby spring provided the household water. The streets were dirt—and turned to mud with the winter rains. Residents traveled from one place to another by foot, horseback, horse-drawn buggy, or the railroad that stopped at the foot of Depot Street.

Most families had their own cows for milk and chickens—for eggs and frying. Families heated their homes with wood-burning stoves for the most part, although some burned coal. Wood also fueled the cookstove, which accounted for tall wood piles in the back yard as winter approached.

Refrigerators were still a vision of the future. Ice boxes, meanwhile, provided sufficient cooling capacity for the hot summer months. Some ice would come from Scott's Mill Pond—enough to last many households all summer. As the late William E. Sandidge Jr. once recalled it, a two-horse wagon pulled a load of ice up Scott's Hill to ice boxes in town.

Such was life in the little village one hundred years ago. As one might expect in the county seat, there were general stores, a bank, several doctors, a dentist, a civil engineer, a gunsmith, a hardware store, and nearly a dozen attorneys.

Among the other various business enterprises were saloons or taverns, as many as fifteen of them, according to Paul Wailes III. Other sources put the number at seven or fewer, with one in each of the two hotels, the Central Hotel and the Virginia House. Many of the saloons were in the area of the depot, where travelers would have a drink—or two—while awaiting the trains.

It is fair to suppose that the village's saloons (and the behavior they encouraged) helped to spur the incorporation of the town of Amherst. Under this theory, the town incorporated so it could regulate the saloons

9

O. V. HANGER

The name O. Victor Hanger appears frequently during any perusal of the town's early records. He was the town's first clerk and served on Town Council for thirty years.

O.V. Hanger
From *Men of Mark*

Hanger was born in Augusta County in 1875 and came to Amherst in 1897 to run a hardware business. By 1902, he took the first steps that would lead him to be prominently identified in Virginia political circles. That year he became a State Senate committee clerk and in 1908 was appointed assistant clerk of the Senate. Four years later, he became clerk of the Senate, a position he would hold until 1926.

The legislature was truly part-time in those days, so he could fulfill his duties in Amherst while serving the citizen legislature for forty-five to sixty days a year, every other year.

Following his Senate service, Hanger filled a number of posts in the state Democratic Party, including heading up Harry F. Byrd's successful primary campaign in 1926. For more than twenty years he was secretary of the Democratic Committee of Amherst County.

O.V. Hanger died at his home in Amherst in January 1940. It was written after his death that he "was never too tired to be of service to his fellow man and at the same time efficient and progressive in his duties. [He] holds a lofty place in the annals of the Commonwealth's development."

—*Robert Wimer*

through a series of laws and taxes. People in the village needed police protection from the brawls that would erupt on occasion inside and outside the barrooms. And the most efficient way to provide that protection and get a grip on the rising number of saloons was to incorporate the village as a town.

The record bears the "saloon theory" out. Following the General Assembly's approval of the village as an incorporated town, the new town council dealt quickly with the saloons and other emporiums that dispensed alcohol.

The council's first meeting on June 28, 1910, with C. L. Scott presiding as mayor, took care of such housekeeping duties as electing Thomas Whitehead as town counsel. It also approved the sum of $15 a month for a town sergeant, beginning on July 1, 1910.

By the next week, the council settled into the serious work of making Amherst a better place to live and work. From the beginning, the council made it clear it wanted no one with concealed weapons walking about the unpaved streets.

Central Hotel, a likely spot for one of Amherst's taverns.
Paul Wailes III photo

Conviction of such an offense could bring a fine of not less than $25 nor more than $100.

The council then moved to enact a section of new ordinances under the general title of "Peace, Good Order and Morals." It was a voluminous series of laws that generally sought to maintain order in the town.

Among the prohibited offenses, violation of which generally carried a $5 fine upon conviction, were disorderly noises, public drunkenness, throwing stones or discharging arrows, playing games in the street, and cockfighting.

Obscene language and drawings were also off limits, with a $10 fine for each conviction. Houses of "ill fame" were deemed particularly offensive and anyone who kept one for the purpose of prostitution could be sentenced to six months in jail and fined not less than $50.

The town fathers also took a dim view of daytime bathing "in the pond or creek" without wearing a bathing suit. The fine for conviction was $2.50 for each offense.

Always in search of potential revenues, as is the case today, one of the first ordinances to be approved imposed a license tax of $15 a day on dog, pony, and trained animal shows, including Wild West shows.

Town residents were allowed to keep livestock, but the animals had to be confined. Dogs had to be licensed and the owners who thumbed their noses at the law were fined $2.50 a day.

The town ordinance did not tolerate animal abuse. Anyone convicted of torturing animals could be fined not less than $5 nor more than $10 for each offense. Anyone caught shooting a yard sparrow, martin, wren or other bird was fined $1 for each offense. The law excepted domestic pigeons killed by their owners.

On July 19, 1910, the council approved its first budget, which came in at $1,155, including $255 for salaries. Among the taxes approved to cover the expenses was a poll tax for males, age twenty-one and older, of fifty cents. The real estate tax rate was

The original name of the town of Amherst was **Five Oaks.**

Looking south on Main Street in the early 1900s.
Joy Graybill photo

11

TOWN SEAL

The town seal almost used the majestic Blue Ridge Mountain ridge line west of Amherst as its theme. That idea, however, was rejected because it represented an area outside of the town's corporate limits.

Walter Creau, a commercial artist from Cleveland, Ohio, came up with the initial idea. As a short history on the town's Web site details it, Creau was visiting his wife's uncle, James Bigby Davis, the town clerk in the mid-1960s. Creau became responsible for creating the seal.

It was later suggested that the Amherst Courthouse be used on the official seal for the town. During that era, a large letter "A" had been attached to a radio antenna behind the courthouse. Although some folks in town disdained the "A" as something less than tasteful, it became part of the current seal—rising behind the stately courthouse. The original seal, which includes the town's date of incorporation, can be seen on the wall of the council chambers in Town Hall.

thirty cents per $100 of assessed valuation and personal property was the same.

In the category of business licenses, the council put the saloons and billiard halls on notice that their services were not especially appreciated—and that if they wanted to stay in business, it would cost them. While the annual business license tax for attorneys, doctors, dentists, engineers and most merchants was $5 to $10, the business license tax on saloons was $100. The council indicated its displeasure with the billiard halls, imposing an additional tax of $50 on each billiard table.

By August of that first year, the council had imposed a 6 mph speed limit for automobiles on the town's streets, although the number of vehicles was not considered significant. The following June, the council made it clear it would enforce the speed limit by authorizing the mayor to purchase an automobile stop watch for the town sergeant at a price not to exceed $10.

And in October 1910, the council approved the town's first set of street lights. They consisted of coal oil (kerosene) fueled lamps with a timing device on them that would allow the lamps to be illuminated at thirty minutes after sundown and to be extinguished at 11 p.m. The council ordered thirty lamps at a cost of $3.50 each. The posts cost an additional thirty-five cents each, but included putting them in the ground.

Within the first two years, the council also laid the groundwork for such important infrastructure as water and sewer lines, street lights, telegraph lines and a $300 contribution toward construction of the new $10,000 high school.

In those first years, nonetheless, the council stuck to its battle against alcohol, which it had deemed the number one troublemaker within the town limits. By May 1913, it had approved a resolution declaring liquor a public nuisance.

Only two establishments that would have found themselves at odds with that Town Council of old exist in the town today. And no one has suggested recently that either Travelers Restaurant in the Ye Old Travelers Coffee Shop building or the Briar Patch on the south end of town are the cause of any unruly behavior. Such is life at the entrance to the town's second century.

Subsequent councils throughout the town's one-hundred-year history have sought to meet what they considered to be the principal needs of town residents. For the most part, they have succeeded. For those councils that did not meet the expectations of the people, no matter the circumstances, the people had the last say at the next election. That's the strength of a representative government that has served the town well during the past century. ∞

Amherst Circuit Court jury on porch of Central Hotel where they often went for meals. Sheriff John Beard stands at extreme left. Standing back row, fourth from left, Gilbert E. Bowman; sixth from left, Elias Rhodes. Front row, starting with third from left: John W. Johnson, Tom Shrader, Nat Stinnett and Henry Burford.
Amherst County Historical Museum photo

Charles H. Joubert's new Haynes car was the first car in Amherst in 1907. From left, Hester Scott Wailes, Mr. Ashley, Mary Scott, Bessie Scott, Charles Joubert, Victor von Gemmingen.
Paul Wailes III photo

14

Connections

Construction crew at work on Southern Railway bridge over the Buffalo River, north of Amherst, in 1915.
Peggy Page photo

PUBLIC SERVICES GREW WITH BIRTH OF TOWN

By Robert C. Wimer

Essential to living in the town of Amherst are the variety of public services that made life a bit more civilized for its residents. In the early days, none of those basic services, such as running water, sewage treatment, electricity, telephone and paved roads were available.

It's not the most exciting part of the little town's history, but those water and sewer lines and roads and electric power lines were just as necessary in the early years as they are today.

The first reference to water and lighting for the town comes in the Town Council's minutes of April 1, 1913, when there was mention of a bond issue for those services. The first water system is believed to have been completed around 1925 with construction of a tank behind the site of the present Catholic church on South Main Street. That system supplied water to Main Street, Garland Avenue and down to the railway depot. The source of the water was Tribulation Creek west of town.

To supplement the water supply, Town Council in 1933 approved a project that created a reservoir about three miles west on Kenmore Road. A line was dug by hand from there to a ground-level tank on Kenmore that's still visible. The fresh mountain water flowed by gravity to the tank and was then pumped up the hill to the above-ground tank.

Paul Wailes III, the town's unofficial historian, recalls that critics of the project, which was paid for in part by the federal government's Works Progress Administration, said it would never generate enough water to supply the town. It didn't work in the long run, but served the town on an interim basis.

The town's source of water eventually shifted to the Buffalo River, where water is taken in and pumped to the water treatment plant on Grandview Drive, a plant that has been expanded over the years. It currently has a production capacity of one million gallons a day and the town has two storage tanks that hold one million gallons each.

Sewer

In the early days, sewage disposal got no fancier than an outhouse for most town residents. With the inauguration of the town's water

17

system, septic systems replaced some of those outhouses or privies. The first sewer system—or wastewater collection system as it is referred to these days—was constructed in the mid-1930s by the federal government's Works Progress Administration. That service covered downtown or a portion of town that included Main Street, Depot Street, Garland Avenue and west along what is now Route 60.

Service north of Route 60, including North Main Street, was installed in the 1950s; and the interceptor from Sweet Briar College and the Ambriar Shopping Center area to the waste-

Amherst businessman **Joe Goodwin** worked for the American Bridge Company as part of the effort to build the Panama Canal.

water treatment plant was installed in the 1970s.

The first sewage treatment plant was built on a creek near the depot and the Amherst Milling Company. A later treatment plant was located off Whitehead Drive. Today, the town owns and operates the Rutledge Creek treatment plant located behind the Zane G. Snead Industrial Park.

Electricity

By 1920, kerosene lamps and candles gave way to electric lights for some residents. Town Council minutes show that electricity came to Amherst on July 30, 1920, when the council sold a franchise to Vernon M. Bugg for $1 to provide electricity to the town. Later that same day, the council approved the local prohibition ordinance.

Bugg, whose nickname reportedly was "Lightning," agreed to supply electricity to 24 50-watt street lights for $50 a month. He also agreed to offer electricity to homes for $2.50 a month for up to 10 lights. The charge for each additional light was 6 cents.

As the *Amherst New Era-Progress* reported in its Bicentennial Edition, Bugg started business with a second-hand generator on West Court Street. The power came on an hour after sunset and went off one hour after dawn. The lights blinked five minutes before they went off.

Six months later Bugg went out of business. But Walker A. Baldock, owner of Amherst Milling Company, succeeded him. From his plant designed to generate electricity for the mill, he supplied power to 15 customers using water power and a hand-cranked 16-kilowatt diesel generator. Among his employees was

Central Virginia Telephone Corporation with the fleet of repair trucks outside the company's new building on South Main Street.
Amherst New Era-Progress photo

Maurice W. Gannaway, who helped with the wiring for customers. Baldock, who was elected to five terms on Town Council, charged $3 a month for 20 kilowatt hours.

In 1925, Lynchburg Traction and Light Company took over the electrical system that had grown to 30 street lights (which cost the town $66.50 a month) and 400 customers. Lynchburg Traction and Light became part of Appalachian Power Company in 1926. APCo's parent company, American Electric Power, serves the town today.

Telephone system

The town's communications system originated with the telegraph service provided by the depot. From the beginning, that was where messages arrived from and were sent to the outside world. Later, a Mr. Seay operated the first phone company from the depot. By the mid-1920s, L. V. Parr took over the phone company and moved it up to Second Street next to his funeral home. The telephone switchboard was operated from the Parr's home.

The telephone system grew under the Parr's management. By the early 1950s, there were a few private lines, but most of the lines were party lines where as many five or six households were linked together. They could listen in on their neighbor's phone call if they were so disposed, but most did not.

Phone numbers in those days seem odd compared to the standardized area codes and numbers today. One can recall the two-digit phone number of the newspaper office—13. And the number at my residence on Old Stage Road was 97W5.

Those were also the days when the switchboard operator could usually tell you everything that was going on in town. Was she listening in on some of the calls?

Peggy Gregory Lau recalls that she loved to chat with the switchboard operators. She said her favorite was Mary Clark, who married Hiter (Buck) Coffey, one of the phone company's linesmen and repairmen. "Any time I was scolded at home or felt lonely, I knew a friendly and sympathetic voice was as close as the telephone."

She adds that the operator must have recognized her voice when she wanted to call her grandmother. "I did not have to provide a number ... I would just tell her I wanted to talk to granny and she would know where to connect the call."

By 1954, the Amherst Telephone Co. had converted to a dial system and was bought by Mr. and Mrs. L. John Denney, who moved here from New Jersey. Denney brought a wide array of experience to the little telephone company and vowed to double the number of subscribers

Civilian Conservation Corps work crew constructing bridge on Route 60 west of Amherst in the 1930s.
Amherst County Historical Museum photo

to as many as 1,400.

The prefix for the fledgling dial system was Whitehall 6, which is the same prefix for local numbers used today—946.

In forming Central Virginia Telephone Co., Denney reached his goal of 1,400 subscribers and along the way became mayor of the town in 1960. He became one of the first of a number

THE CIRCLE
ONE OF NATION'S OLDEST

The traffic circle at the intersection of U.S. Routes 60 and 29 was born of necessity. Stories abound that folks would gather on busy weekends and watch the accidents occur as vehicles sought to get through the busy intersection that was a major link for vehicles passing in any direction through town.

The circle was designed in 1936 by W. M. Jeffries, an engineer who highway officials say might have been years ahead of his time. Construction began shortly thereafter. It is believed to be the oldest traffic circle, roundabout as they are called today, in Virginia and one of the oldest in the nation.

Walter Pribble, a senior transportation planner with the Virginia Department of Transportation, said in 2006 that according to state records, "the Amherst traffic circle pre-dates the official modern roundabout in this country by more than 50 years." The first modern roundabout in the United States, he said, was built in Nevada in 1990.

The state has turned to the modern roundabout more often to enhance safety at busy intersections and reduce delays for motorists.

At one point in the circle's long history, it contained a confusing array of traffic signs pointing motorists north, east, south and west, along with the cities and towns that could be found along the way.

Today, it is far more attractive, thanks to the cooperative efforts of the Village Garden Club and town officials. An 850-gallon basin water fountain was installed in the center of the circle in June 2006. The flowers planted around it and maintained by the garden club members have drawn rave reviews for their color and abundance. Lights at Christmas have also drawn favorable attention to the circle, making it one of the town's most memorable and enduring landmarks.

of business executives who sought to breathe new life into the town. He succeeded for the most part. With the exception of two years between 1970 and 1972, he served as mayor until his death in 1983.

CVTC eventually became part of Continental Telephone Co., which had its regional headquarters in Amherst in the mid-1960s. Continental later combined with General Telephone and Electronics, which eventually merged with Chesapeake and Potomac. Verizon serves the town today.

Roads

By the time the town was incorporated in 1910, the railroad provided most of the transportation to and from Amherst for both freight and passengers. In earlier days, stagecoaches offered long-distance travel over dirt roads that became dusty in the summer and quagmires during the winter seasons of snow and rain.

Travel time puts the difference between the horse-drawn stage and the steam-driven iron horse in perspective. Passengers could go from Lynchburg to Washington, D.C. (with a stop in Amherst) in eight hours, while the same trip by stage took three days. The "local" stage coach

Looking south at Amherst traffic circle in 2010. The seasonal plantings are maintained by the Village Garden Club.
Paul Wailes III photo

20

ran between Amherst and Lynchburg once a day, with the one-way fare set at $1.50. It continued operation until about 1920.

The maintenance and construction of streets became an important part of the town's life, a fact reflected in the first town budget that provided $550 for streets. That was nearly one-third of the $1,700 budget for 1911. Most folks traveled around town by horse and buggy or wagon. Only a handful of automobiles were registered in the town at the time, including the first automobile, which belonged to Charles H. Joubert. His new Haynes car arrived at the depot in 1907 and was stored during the winter at the Wailes' house on Garland Avenue.

The original Route 60 was known as Route 13. It ran east–west and was referred to as Monitor Road. East of Amherst, Route 13 went down Depot Street past the train station and Amherst Milling Company.

The north–south road through town was referred to as Route 18. The two roads intersected at what is now the traffic light at Main and Second streets. Route 18 between Amherst and Lynchburg was the first in the area to become a road paved with tar and gravel. At the time, such a road was referred to as a macadam road—a significant improvement over the existing dirt and gravel roads.

The main thoroughfares through town were redesignated in 1932 as U.S. Route 60 and U.S. Route 29 to conform to the federal highway numbering system. And later in that decade, the main road through town was paved.

Public services offered by the town have come a long way in the century since it was incorporated. Water, sewer, paved streets, electricity and telephones are hallmarks of life today in Amherst. But, as current members of Town Council will tell you, the services come at a price—part of the cost of living with modern conveniences. ∽

Welby Bailey served the town as director of public utilities for twenty-seven years between 1963 and 1990. He was legendary in his knowledge of the town water and sewer system.
The News & Advance photo

The caption on this postcard identifies this as "a good road in Amherst."
Amherst County Historical Museum photo

21

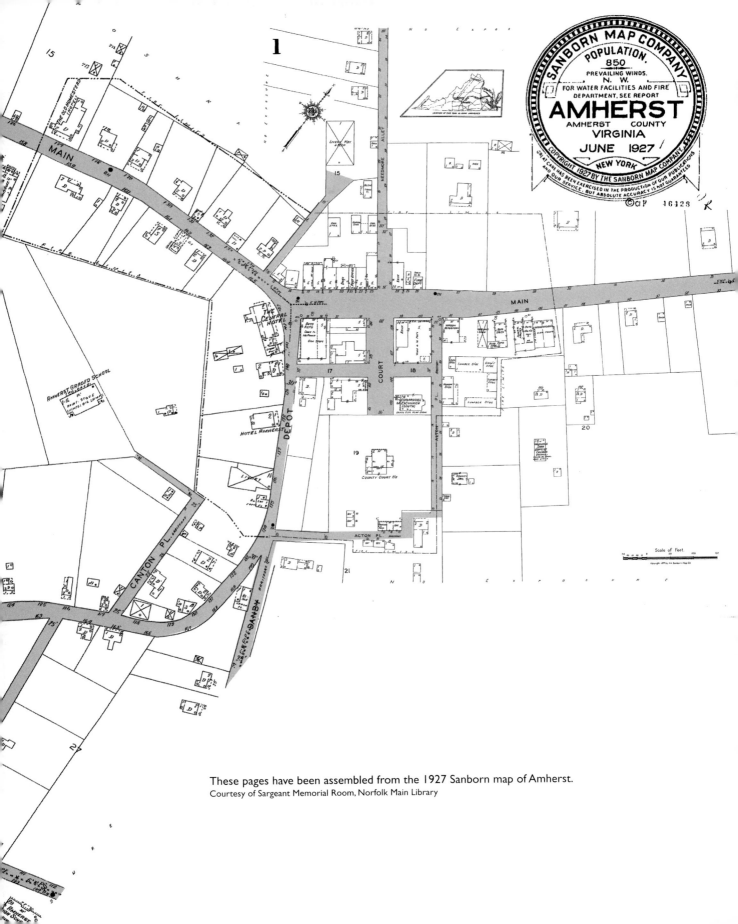

These pages have been assembled from the 1927 Sanborn map of Amherst.
Courtesy of Sargeant Memorial Room, Norfolk Main Library

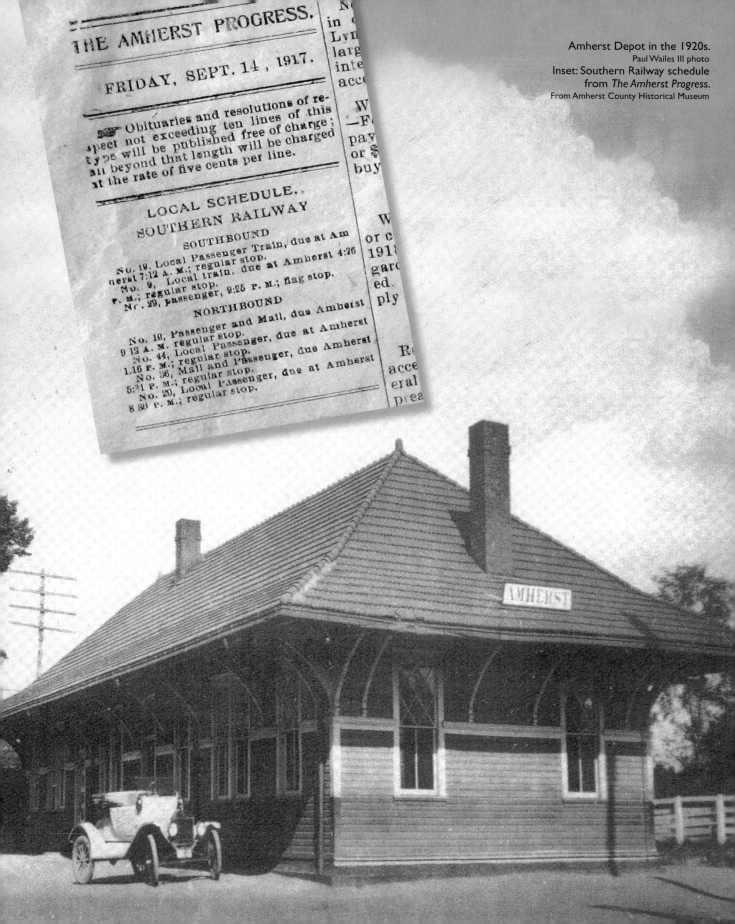

THE AMHERST PROGRESS.

FRIDAY, SEPT. 14, 1917.

☞ Obituaries and resolutions of respect not exceeding ten lines of this type will be published free of charge; all beyond that length will be charged at the rate of five cents per line.

LOCAL SCHEDULE.
SOUTHERN RAILWAY

SOUTHBOUND

No. 19, Local Passenger Train, due at Amherst 7:12 A. M.; regular stop.

No. 9, Local train, due at Amherst 4:26 P. M.; regular stop.

No. 29, passenger, 9:25 P. M.; flag stop.

NORTHBOUND

No. 10, Passenger and Mail, due Amherst 9 13 A. M. regular stop.

No. 44, Local Passenger, due at Amherst 1.16 P. M.; regular stop.

No. 36, Mail and Passenger, due Amherst 5:31 P. M.; regular stop.

No. 20, Local Passenger, due at Amherst 8 30 P. M.; regular stop.

Amherst Depot in the 1920s.
Paul Wailes III photo
Inset: Southern Railway schedule from *The Amherst Progress.*
From Amherst County Historical Museum

TRAINS KEPT TOWN
RUNNING ON TIME

By H. L. Hansberry III

By the time Amherst was incorporated, railroad service had been a fixture for half a century. In 1860, the Orange and Alexandria was extended from Charlottesville to Lynchburg, providing access to the northeast as well as connections to Richmond and points west.

Traditionally, railroads are a boom or bust business, and the Orange and Alexandria was no exception. Through reorganizations and mergers, the Orange and Alexandria subsequently became Virginia Midland, Richmond and Danville, and finally, in 1894, the Southern Railway. In 1982, the Southern merged with the Norfolk and Western to form the Norfolk Southern which still passes through today.

For an appreciation of the railroad of the early 20th century, one must put its multiple roles into the context of both historical events and the alternative forms of transportation and communication available.

In 1910, few automobiles were registered in Amherst. The quality of roads was poor, often impassable in inclement weather. The statewide speed limit was 20 miles per hour—even slower in towns. The primary east–west and north–south routes followed circuitous routes before being replaced in the 1930s by current U.S. highways, 29 and 60, rendering the train as the most viable option for business or pleasure.

A 1917 Southern Railway schedule shows seven daily departures from Amherst. One could board a parlor car or sleeper at the foot of Depot Street and be whisked off in relative luxury to then-exotic places such as New York City.

A small community grew up around the Amherst Depot, with several homes and businesses in the immediate area. Until the incorporation of Amherst, the location of the depot was actually called Dearborn, with its own post office in "Jeweler" Smith's store.

Depot Street was a busy thoroughfare into town. Those disembarking the trains found libations at nearby taverns and lodging closer to town. During the Depression, hobos hopped trains, jumped off before being caught, and wandered to nearby homes looking for meals and work.

It was not uncommon for Amherst residents to ride to Lynchburg to buy groceries, then return

Postmark from the Dearborn, Va. Post Office
Courtesy of Nancy McDearmon

Dispatcher's desk at Amherst Depot communications center. Amherst County Historical Museum photo

that afternoon. En route to Lynchburg, "locals" made stops at Sweet Briar, McIvor, Monroe, and Winesap.

Some students rode the train to Amherst for high school. Thomas and John Pettyjohn boarded at McIvor on Sunday evening to ride to Amherst, where they stayed with their relatives, the Meeks family. They returned home near Monroe on Friday.

From 1839 until 1975, the Railway Express Agency (REA) and its predecessor filled the roles now held by UPS and Fed Ex. Its privately owned cars provided timely delivery of the goods needed for small town life, everything from auto and tractor parts to baby chicks and farm animals. Farmers used the service to ship fresh milk to market. Billy Wydner relates the story of going to the agent to pick up a coon dog ordered through a mail order catalog. In small towns, station agents served as REA representatives.

For about a century, beginning near the end of the Civil War, many trains contained railway post office cars (RPOs) carrying clerks who sorted mail en route. The local post office sent a courier with a sack of outgoing mail and returned with inbound mail. Express trains threw off a mail sack and "hooked" the outbound sack suspended from a tall pole a few feet from the tracks. This service afforded small communities along the tracks timely and consistent postal service. Paul Wailes III remembers his grandfather's receiving a letter one morning postmarked "Wall Street NYC" the previous morning. Occasionally, a mail bag took an aberrant bounce and ended up under the wheels, with the sack's contents being strewn in every direction.

In the early 20th century, station agents served as representatives of the Western Union Corporation. With no television, radio, or telephone in existence, the telegraph was the only method of rapid transmission of information. Many an Amherst family learned of important news by a telegram posted on the front door.

As Amherst has evolved over the past century, so, too, have the needs of the town's businesses.

In 1907, when the Jouberts bought Amherst's first automobile, it was delivered by train. This practice continued as Babcock Chevrolet received inventory by rail until the 1950s.

For years farmers drove their cattle down the dirt streets of Amherst to a cattle pen located directly across the tracks from the station to await shipment to market. Through freight trains paused here to unload livestock for food, water, and exercise in compliance with existing rules before being reloaded and shipped to their destination.

Since their inception, the railroads have excelled at transportation of bulk commodities. For decades, Mays Farmers Service received carloads of fertilizer, lime, and hay. Hill Hardware unloaded coal by hand into trucks, which carried it to feed the furnaces of Amherst residences. Up until the 1950s, wheat grown by local farmers was shipped by rail to mills.

Following the destruction inflicted by Hurricane Camille in 1969, the Southern Railway transported construction materials for rebuilding the many damaged roads and bridges.

In 1977, the spur track to Buffalo Forge was still in place, but the shipping of air handling equipment was largely by truck. This track was removed in the 1980s, leaving the town without a rail customer for several years. Rail service returned to Amherst when First Brands opened in 1991 to produce "Glad Bags." This plant, now owned by Clorox, regularly receives covered hoppers laden with plastic pellets.

Of all the changes in the past century, perhaps none has been greater than the decline in railroad employment and its subsequent economic impact. Because of Amherst's proximity to major railroad facilities at Monroe and Gladstone, many local families received paychecks from either the Southern Railway or the Chesapeake and Ohio. As time passed, increased mechanization of track maintenance, closure of stations, and changes in work rules

- **Marvin E. "Monk" Robertson was the conductor on the first train to pass over the newly rebuilt Tye River Bridge after Hurricane Camille.**
- **Only minutes before "The Old 97" departed Monroe for its fateful trip south, as immortalized in song, it passed through Amherst.**
- **Train engineers developed distinctive ways of blowing the whistle. Each had his signature technique, which nearby family and friends could recognize as the train passed.**
- **The first regularly scheduled diesel-powered train to pass through Amherst, The Southerner, made its inaugural run on February 27, 1941. Some Amherst students recall sitting on a bank below the school watching it.**
- **The Amherst station now on U.S. 60 was built in 1913, replacing another built by the Orange and Alexandria. The station was moved from Depot Street to its present location on January 25, 2008.**

led to the inexorable erosion of railroad jobs.

In recent years, people have reawakened to the fact that rail is inherently an energy efficient and environmentally sound way to move both goods and people. It is not inconceivable that at some point in the future, one may be able to amble down Depot Street and reach one's destination much as people did in 1910. ☜

Dr. Hansberry practiced dentistry in Amherst for 30 years. He has been interested in railroads for as long as he can remember.

Devoid of its roofing tiles, the Amherst depot appears forlorn as the Norfolk Southern local passes in December 2007, barely a month before relocation to the Route 60 site.
H. L. Hansberry III photo

NEWSPAPERS HAVE
SERVED AMHERST SINCE 1881

By Robert C. Wimer

From the beginning, the village that became the town of Amherst has been served by at least one weekly newspaper. Between 1903 and 1924, the little town had two weekly papers, a circumstance that undoubtedly provided lively competition for news and advertising.

But that was to be expected in the county seat of a thriving community where the number of lawyers nearly exceeded the merchants and other tradesmen.

The village that was to become the county seat originally bore the name Five Oaks, a stop on the stage run from Lynchburg to Charlottesville. It was conveniently located near the center of the new Amherst County that was formed when the original county was divided, resulting in the creation of Nelson County to the north in 1807. With the name changed to Amherst and construction of a new courthouse, the village began to grow, reaching a population of 550 by 1882.

Henry Aubrey Strode, who started Kenmore as a college preparatory school for boys and went on to become the first president of Clemson University, founded the village's first weekly newspaper, *The New Era*, in 1881.

Indeed it was a new era. By that time, as Sherrie and William McLeRoy observed in their history of Amherst County, the county seat

28

EDITOR'S INDEPENDENCE TARNISHED ON OCCASION

An adage in the newspaper business is that reporters and editors try to maintain a certain independence from the people and organizations they cover. On a small weekly newspaper in a small community such as Amherst, that is not always possible.

I discovered that the hard way.

While working as managing editor of the *Amherst New Era-Progress* in the early 1970s I found it difficult to maintain the independence that I thought should be a part of the job.

Why? There were two reasons. First, my boss, J. Bernard "Mac" McDearmon was a member of the Amherst County Board of Supervisors, the local governing body that I regularly covered. Second, my mother, Elizabeth F. Wimer, who for years was also managing editor of the newspaper, had retired and was appointed to the county school board, another body that I covered on a regular basis.

Mac and I usually viewed stories coming out of the supervisors' meetings with the same eye. That is, we pretty much agreed on what the most important items of business were to our readers. There were times, however, when I would find out something that was coming before the supervisors that my news judgment told me warranted a story before it got to the governing body.

In several instances, which included the possibility of a new business or new employer coming to town, Mac persuaded me that it would be better to sit on the story because the story might have a negative effect on any negotiations taking place behind the scenes. I disagreed with him, but deferred to his position both as a supervisor—and my publisher. After all, he authorized my pay checks.

In those days, the school board and supervisors didn't always put the best interests of the students and teachers ahead of their political interests. Many residents will remember those days when the supervisors, who tried to control the school system's purse strings, would vote against programs they didn't like by withholding money from the school budget.

That was illegal, of course, because the supervisors could not dictate to the school system where—and where not—to spend money appropriated by the county. But that did not stop them from trying.

And that put me in the uncomfortable position of trying to present both sides to our readers, while at the same placating Mac and my mother, both of whom were good advocates for their side of the issue.

A case in point was a budget item for special education in the county. Public education for students who were either mentally or physically challenged—or both—was relatively new to Virginia and to the county. Mac and a majority of the supervisors did not believe in spending as much money on special education students as the school administrators had proposed.

The school board knew it was the right thing to do, and insisted on keeping the expenditure in the budget. And when the supervisors sought to reduce the budget item for special education, school administrators, with the school board's approval, resorted to some chicanery that divvied up the budgeted amount into several other parts of the spending plan the next year.

When I discovered that—and reported it—Mac was furious. The school superintendent at the time was not one of his favorite people in the first place and Mac didn't disguise his feelings about him within the confines of the newspaper office on Second Street. My mother supported the proposal to spend more for special education, so I was put right in the middle of the debate.

The school board, as I recall, eventually won that battle. But it was not one of the high points of cooperation between the two boards—cooperation that should have focused on the students and their needs and not on any personal battle between the supervisors and the school board and administration.

Working with Mac and his wife, Louise, was an interesting experience and I learned a lot about the newspaper business that I had not encountered in my previous experience with *The Daily Progress* in Charlottesville. However, I never really mastered cheering for one side or the other in the course of my duties as an editor and reporter. Such independence comes naturally, I suppose, to most newspaper people. But not all, as I discovered at the *New Era-Progress*.

—Robert Wimer

J.B. McDearmon
Amherst New Era-Progress photo

Elizabeth F. Wimer
Bob Wimer photo

Top: Hughsie Penn operates the press that printed the *Amherst New Era-Progress* in the basement of Amherst Publishing Company on Second Street.
Marianna Penn photo

J.B. McDearmon, publisher of the *Amherst New Era-Progress*, explains typesetting for students from E.C. Glass. Setting the type is Page Stinnett, long-time employee. At that time, Amherst Publishing Company was located at the corner of Main and Star Streets.
McDearmon family photo

During that time, Clarence J. Campbell, the judge who gained fame for horse whipping a minister on the courthouse steps, also served as editor of *The New Era*, the name of which changed around 1890 to the *Amherst New Era*.

A second weekly newspaper hit the streets in 1903, *The Amherst Progress*, published by one F. J. Harris about whom little is known. He and his successors did manage to compete with the *Amherst New Era* for slightly more than two decades, when the two papers merged in 1924, creating the *Amherst New Era-Progress*, the name of the paper that serves the town and county today.

Among the village's residents during that era was Thomas Whitehead, who founded *The Daily Advance* in Lynchburg in 1880. He had been editor of *The News* in Lynchburg for a number of years before starting *The Daily Advance*, which was eventually bought by Robert Henry Glass, the father of Carter Glass, in 1893.

Lucian H. Shrader, a lawyer and member of the Virginia House of Delegates, bought the *Amherst New Era-Progress* in 1924 and formed the Amherst Publishing Co. with the formation of the *Buckingham News* and purchase of the *Nelson County Times*. He and his wife, Bess, were joint owners and editors of the three county newspapers.

Shrader went on to become trial justice of Amherst County in 1938, a position he served until the time of his death in 1976. Trial justice was roughly the equivalent of today's general district court judge.

The newspapers changed hands again when the Shraders sold them to two Lynchburg newspapermen, Gilbert R. Haile, city editor of *The News*, and J. Bernard McDearmon, state editor of *The News*. That was in August 1946.

McDearmon and his wife, Louise, ran the newspapers from a building just off the

had become a "flourishing little place" with an economy based on tobacco. In 1882, there were eight general stores, five lawyers and one saloon. Two doctors, a blacksmith, a real estate salesman and two carpenters also served the village.

Less than a decade later, Amherst had added the county's only listed bank, a dentist, a civil engineer, a gunsmith and hardware store, several more doctors and 11 of the county's 17 attorneys. The number of saloons had increased to five, including ones at the two hotels, the Central Hotel on Main Street and the Virginia House.

Courthouse Green in Amherst for nearly a decade. Like the Shraders before them, they also printed several high school and college newspapers, along with filling job printing orders that included stationery and envelopes, posters and whatever else needed to be printed in great quantities. It was the job printing that gave the newspaper office and plant the term many used for it then and still do today—the printing office.

From the deteriorating building near the Courthouse, the newspaper moved to a structure on Main Street that had served as the Golden Glow Dairy, taking the old flat-bed press that could print only eight pages at a time with it. The former dairy retail outlet, which had a soda fountain that attracted teenagers after school during the 1950s, remained the home of the *New Era-Progress* until 1969 when the McDearmons moved the newspaper to the new brick building on Second Street, where it remains today.

With that move, the paper's owners bought a larger press from the Farmville newspaper— one that could print more than eight pages at a time. The company eventually bought a newer press that could accommodate two sections in one printing. Keene Brown joined Mac as a part owner of the newspaper when the new building was constructed on Second Street. Keene wrote editorials for the paper for several years in the early 1970s.

In October 1981, the *Winchester Evening Star* bought the Amherst Publishing Co. and its two papers. J. B. "Mac" McDearmon, who had owned and published the papers for 35 years, said at the time he was "tired of it and it was time to get out." Among the *Winchester Evening Star's* stockholders was former U.S. Sen. Harry F. Byrd Jr.

The Byrd Newspapers published the Amherst and Nelson weeklies for two decades until they sold them in May 2001 to Media General, the Richmond-based current owner of the *Amherst New Era-Progress.* Media General owned the daily papers in Lynchburg and Charlottesville, and Media General officials said it made sense to increase their holdings in Central Virginia with the two weekly papers.

Among the changes brought on by improved technology in the newspaper business has been the consolidation of printing the regional papers at one location—in Lynchburg. That's more efficient, certainly, but surely not as colorful as that old flat-bed press that sounded like a chugging "African Queen" when the electric motor was switched on. ∞

POLLY THE PARROT

A young Robbie D. Mantiply with her parrot, Polly.
Robbie Howell photo

Robbie D. (Mantiply) Howell remembers accompanying her father, Rob, when he delivered groceries in the mid-1930s, and one of his customers was Effie Wills, at the south end of town. As a young girl, Robbie was especially enamored of Mrs. Wills' parrot "Polly." As luck would have it, Mrs. Wills offered Robbie the parrot, because the parrot and one of Mrs. Wills' boarders had an adversarial relationship. Either the parrot or the boarder had to go.

With considerable prodding of her parents, Robbie was able to seal the deal. Polly moved into the Mantiply household and quickly became a "member of the family" for more than thirty years. She was a beautiful green, with red and gold. Her diet consisted primarily of sunflower seeds. She didn't like water for a bath, but would douse her head occasionally in her water dish.

Polly was rather talkative with an interesting vocabulary. Polly was a great companion for all members of the family, both indoors and out, sitting quietly under his chair as Mr. Mantiply's health declined in the late '60s.

Among Polly's pronouncements would be "Praise God!," although one day when a neighbor dropped by, Polly exclaimed "Great God!" She also would scream "Mama" often, or call the dog "Billy." Funerals in the nearby cemetery were sometimes interrupted by Polly, who would be outside in her cage. One man walking into the cemetery kept turning around, saying, "Who's that hollering at me?"

Polly died quietly around 1970 after many years of entertaining chatter.

HOUSE CALLS ON HORSEBACK

By Patty Walton Turpin

D r. Reuben Barnes Ware was born in 1873 on Indian Creek in Amherst County. When he was growing up, one of his younger sisters died because her family was unable to get her to a doctor in a timely fashion. At that point, my grandfather made the decision to become a doctor.

Dr. Ware began his education in a one-room school at Ivy Hill, and then went to the College of William and Mary. Those years were interrupted for him to earn money to continue

Medical student R. B. Ware, center, joins classmates at the Medical College of Virginia in the early 1890s in study of a cadaver.
Patty Turpin photo

toward his goal. He saved his money as a teacher in Amherst County and completed his medical degree at the Medical College of Virginia in 1895.

When the Medical College needed cadavers for anatomy study, legend has it that the janitor, Chris, under cover of darkness, would go to the graves of the unknown and unclaimed in the Richmond public cemetery. He would carry a cadaver in a big barrel back to MCV. If questioned by the authorities as to the contents of the barrel, his reply was "cabbage, sir."

Dr. Ware began his practice in Lowesville in 1895 and married Birdie Drummond that same year. They would raise ten children.

My grandfather served in the House of Delegates from 1901 to 1903. He chose not to run for another term because he thought his medical practice was more important. Dr. Julian Woodson of Lowesville took over Dr. Ware's practice during Ware's absence while in Richmond.

In the early years, Dr. Ware had to ride horseback to get to his patients. He kept two good saddle horses so a fresh one would be available. Once he had to travel through a heavy sleet storm, arriving with his feet frozen to the stirrups. A family member had to assist him in removing ice from his boots so he could dismount.

At times my grandfather would have to spend the night at a patient's home because of the distance on horseback. One evening at a home visit, the children of the family were so excited to learn their doctor would be spending the night because it meant they would have gravy for breakfast.

My grandfather said at the beginning of his practice many people did not understand the need for sanitary precautions. He therefore treated many cases of dysentery and typhoid fever. It was a struggle to educate people to take the necessary precautions to stay healthy. He gave the first antitoxin serum to be used in the Lowesville area.

During his fifty-plus years of practice, Dr. Ware delivered more than 3,000 babies. The names Reuben, Barnes, and Ware were used many times for a baby to honor my grandfather. He answered every call he could. He was there for all people in need and never asked if they could pay before a visit. Many times he received produce for his services. He rarely spent a night without being called out in the evening. He had gotten up, dressed to go out, returned, and gotten up again—as many as seven times in one night.

In 1912, Dr. Ware moved his family to the town of Amherst. He practiced out of his home on Main Street near the circle. My cousin Bob Ware and Richard Coffey, who visited the Ware home as youngsters, said the Ware household was like a movie production. Mrs. Ware was the director with people coming and going in different directions while she managed all the various family activities, and Dr. Ware tended to his patients.

Patients stayed in my grandfather's home. An elderly woman and some young boys had been bitten by a rabid dog. They were to be given shots over a period of ten days. The infected people all lived out in the country, so, to save time for other patients as well, these folks remained in the Ware home to receive their daily shots.

My grandfather owned one of the first three automobiles in Amherst. He had a reputation for his terrible driving ability. One time he drove all the way to Richmond and back in second gear. When L. F. Payne arrived in Amherst as a state trooper, he observed how Dr. Ware would park his car in the business area. The car would be parked in the middle of the street or up on the sidewalk. Payne asked who owned the car. He was quickly told that no court in Virginia could get Dr. Ware to park his car properly.

After my father became ill with TB, my immediate family moved in with my grandfather in 1946. My brother Buddy and I would go on house calls when we were children in the late 1940s. We would ride in the back seat of his car—"Miss Fanny," a 1939 Ford coupe—and would remain in the car during the medical visit.

Page Stinnett recalls how he and his family looked forward to a visit from Dr. Ware. After the medical exam was completed, Dr. Ware would "kick back" and tell many tales. I am sure some were true and others were embellished. It was a well-known fact that Dr. Ware would enjoy a drink or two.

Paul Wailes III remembers my grandfather's ability to just brighten up a room when he walked through the door.

For me to live in a home with someone of my grandfather's enormous stature and dedication was a wonderful experience that has lasted throughout my life. To learn how giving, kind, humorous and loving a true Virginia gentleman can be is a real treasure.

☯

Dr. Reuben B. Ware
From *Men of Mark*

Medical pioneer **Walter Reed** had close relatives who lived in Amherst.

Amherst School in the mid-1930s.
Nancy Marion photo

Living

& Learning

The original name of teams at Amherst High School was the "Rebels."

Top: Amherst Elementary teachers in the mid-1950s: from left, Elsie Ware, Stella Allen, Adelaide Hapala, Edith Evans, Kathleen Proffitt, Elizabeth Wright, Bernice Hunt, Sally Stone, Dolly Payne, Margaret Ware, Louise Cash, and Elizabeth Mantiply.
Amherst County Historical Museum photo

Above: Amherst High School Class of 1942
Paul Wailes III photo

STRICT SCHOOLMARMS
SERVED UP EFFECTIVE LEARNING

By Thurman B. Davis

"I'm gonna be a doctor; what are you gonna be?" Jack Faulconer asked Will Mays at Amherst School, Sept. 8, 1936.

Students knew from an early age that they attended school to "be" something in adulthood. Mays vividly recalled when Faulconer, his first grade classmate, introduced himself and made that proud pronouncement. Faulconer fulfilled his childhood goal, graduating from medical school in 1955 and practicing in the Amherst area over parts of five decades.

Just two years after incorporation of the town, a two-story brick school was built on the corner of Second and Washington streets. A separate elementary school was added in the early 1920s, followed by an auditorium joining the two structures. Before that time, students had been educated in community schools or private homes.

In the earliest years, students from distant parts of the county would sometimes come to school in Amherst, boarding with local families. Students from Monroe could catch a train for the ride to the Amherst Depot just down the hill from the school.

Those who attended the Amherst School in the early decades often spoke of their experiences with two mentors of that era: "Miss Sally" (Robertson) and "Miss Ethel" (Gilbert). They typified the strict but effective "school-marms," laying a strong foundation for students in the lower grades, while demanding high standards for both themselves and their pupils.

Miss Sally's father was an attorney in Amherst. The family valued education and Miss Sally and her sisters started the first library in the town in a room in the basement of Ascension Church, across from their home. The school auditorium, built in 1932, was dedicated to Miss Sally.

Ethel Gilbert was daughter of W. W. Gilbert, Amherst's fourth mayor. Families who have lived in Amherst for multiple generations have heard references to school experiences in the Miss Sally and Miss Ethel eras.

Teachers often required recitation in front of the class—a serious affair where discipline did not seem to be a major problem beyond

37

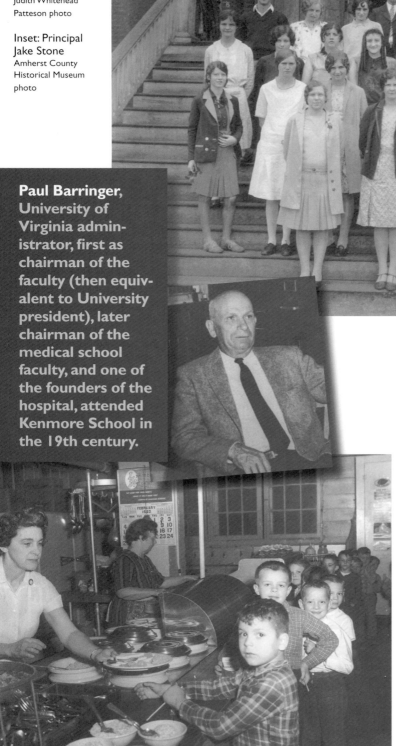

Amherst High School Class of 1929
Judith Whitehead Patteson photo

Inset: Principal Jake Stone
Amherst County Historical Museum photo

Paul Barringer, University of Virginia administrator, first as chairman of the faculty (then equivalent to University president), later chairman of the medical school faculty, and one of the founders of the hospital, attended Kenmore School in the 19th century.

Lunchtime at Amherst school cafeteria, February 1952
Amherst County Historical Museum photo

youthful disagreements, indiscretions, or pranks, as Judith Whitehead Patteson recalled, showing a group picture of the class of 1929.

The twenty-five members of that class, a group of neatly-dressed students on the school steps, were ready to assume their places in the adult world. No training, however, could have prepared them for the challenges that lay ahead in October of that year. They would start their careers and families in the greatest depression this country has ever known.

Students in the 1940s recalled that teacher Lucile Cox made it known on the first day that Latin class was serious business. Students would speak only when questioned by the teacher. A loud slam of the textbook onto the desk provided the exclamation point for her statement.

Teachers took pride in their courses—plane and solid geometry, chemistry, biology, English, Latin, history, and government. Dolly Payne cited Sweet Briar College as an example of an outside resource that teachers and administrators would use to extend students' exposure to other cultures and thoughts. In regional academic competitions, Mrs.

Payne asserted that Amherst acquitted itself well.

Administrators would sometimes supplement students' educational experiences. Joseph Harker, principal in the early 1940s, was especially talented in music, and also introduced students to advanced mathematics.

Jake Stone, arriving as principal in the mid-'40s, taught history and current events, and was instrumental in developing athletic teams. Stone remained as principal until the high school's closure in 1956; he then continued as elementary principal for several years. For many elementary students, the educational experience at the Amherst School was not complete unless they had been summoned to Mr. Stone's office for some transgression.

Ben Smith, class of 1945, began school during the Great Depression and recalled the most signifi-cant event in his high school years—World War II. Dolly Payne said the teachers talked of little else the week following the Pearl Harbor attack. Juanita Iseman Price, class of 1945, remembered friends whose brothers became casualties of war. A more serious atmosphere had been created in all aspects of American life.

Smith stated that students in the war years sometimes were removed from school to offset labor shortages for harvesting apples. There was horseplay as well, with the well-aimed apple nailing a classmate on a nearby orchard ladder.

Students in Amherst could enroll in vocational subjects, with boys in agriculture studies and woodworking and girls in home economics. Harold Higgins' agriculture students developed skills in calculating board feet in timber, dairy judging and crop judging. Home economics students, with their

Faculty and students at Amherst School in 1918.
Patty Turpin photo

CANNERY:

HOT, STEAMY, AND LOUD

An outgrowth of the school's vocational programs was the Amherst County cannery, operated during the summer and fall in a building on the school grounds. Most counties, especially rural ones, provided canneries during the war years and even for several subsequent decades, with some still in operation.

Farmers and gardeners would harvest their crops, load them into baskets or onto trucks, to be brought

garden produce as well as meats in the fall—with a day's tally of cans reaching as many as three to four thousand.

Every fall for a number of years, Ascension Church sold plum pudding at the fall bazaar. The ladies of the church, using their "secret recipe" which included port wine, would combine the ingredients in the church kitchen, then take the rich pudding to the cannery for processing. They produced as many as 500 one-pound cans and sold out on an annual basis.

Those who recalled the activity in the cannery described a hot, steamy, and loud building, buzzing with sounds of shucking, cutting, slicing, or squeezing, accompanied by all the chatter of neighbors helping neighbors, all the while producing vast quantities of supplies for the pantry. Work at the cannery was anticipated enthusiastically, not only as a time for preserving food for the year ahead, but also as a time of great social interaction.

Higgins recalls how some of the women who lived nearby "adopted" the cannery and would help with the work. An especially fond memory was apple butter time, when the ladies would go home, bake biscuits, and bring them back hot, ready for a generous sampling of the apple butter.

Residents prepare vegetables for canning process.
Amherst County Historical Museum photo

to town for canning for the following winter. The only expense incurred by the customers was the cost of the cans.

Vocational teachers oversaw the operation in conjunction with their teaching responsibilities in agriculture (Harold Higgins) and home economics (Mary B. Stinnett, Katherine Feagans, Evelyn Nicholas). Mrs. Marion Burley actually was in charge of the day-to-day operation of the cannery.

A wide range of foods was processed—summer

Various meat products could be canned, and Higgins remembers one such effort for bear meat. Apparently, the meat had spoiled and the cans ultimately exploded. The man's comment regarding his wife's effort was, "I told the old lady you can't keep no 'bar' in a tin can."

—Leah Settle Gibbs

separate building as a laboratory, learned practices for the efficient operation of a home.

Sitting in his living room, Higgins proudly pointed out pieces of furniture made in his wood shop. The Amherst Rotary Club raised money for shop equipment. With a chuckle, he reflected upon a warm spring day, teaching with his windows open, when a disgruntled student stuck his head in from outside and sneered, "Mr. Higgins, I ain't a-skeered of you!" Such are the memories of long-ago school days, seasoned with childhood antics and challenges.

Dolly Payne recalled how class size burgeoned from a manageable number in the 1940s to the "baby boom" of the early '50s with as many as 40 students per class and even 48 in one. Lunch was a challenge for both teachers and students with limited cafeteria facilities.

Amherst High School volleyball team lines the fire escape in 1948. Capt. Jean Jones, Sponsor Edna Loftus. Team: Betty Massie, Robbie Mantiply, Jake Alphin, Margaret Ross, Pearl Lane, Phyllis Hash, Cynthia Irby, Carlene Wilmer, Helen Tsoleas, Helen Lamb, Doris Jones, Bethel Bradley, Alice Nash, Alice Tsoleas. Their record was 5-1 and they won a regional tournament at Lynchburg College by defeating Gladys High School in final.
From 1948 *Lord Geoffrey*, Amherst High School yearbook

Teacher Kathleen Proffitt, back left, and her second grade class at Amherst School in 1953.
McDearmon family photo

Girls often continued their education through one of three avenues: business school for secretarial training, nursing school, or college, predominantly for teacher training. Boys had options of occupations in industrial trades or farming or going to college for professions such as business, law, or medicine. Most of the boys knew that at some point soon they would be called to military service and had to factor that obligation into future plans. Amherst graduates had a number of options in higher education in Virginia, with choices from single-sex or coeducational institutions, both state-supported and private.

The building that now houses the Amherst County Parks and Recreation Department was built for the purpose of housing the Home Economics Department at the old Amherst School.

Regardless of the academic experiences in school, former students of all generations universally noted two sources of amusement: the slanted floor in the auditorium and the spiral fire escape. An open area behind the permanent seats was sloped to accommodate chairs for greater capacity. At other times, that space was used for a variety of events, from volleyball games to dances. The slope always added an interesting dimension to the festivities. The fire escape provided merriment not only during fire drills, but also for recess, as well as for time spent in the neighborhood during non-school hours. The playground and fire escape functioned as a small-time amusement park.

The final chapter of the old high school closed on June 12, 1956, when 28 graduates walked across the stage in the auditorium with its slanted floor. At least half of the class enrolled in higher education and spent subsequent years contributing to the fields of business, law, education, and medicine—not only regionally, but sometimes internationally. Most of the 22 surviving classmates recently came to the 50-year reunion and some have likewise celebrated 50 years of marriage. They expressed no regrets and felt no missed opportunities in being the last of the graduating classes at a small town high school. ∽

Hammett Whitten, a senior in 1912, at the Amherst community school. This building was replaced by the brick school.
Paul Wailes III photo

1915

CLASS ROLL

THEODORE HUBBARD EVANS

ARABELL MOON FALCONER

HENRY EMMETT FULCHER

FELDE VOORHEIS GARLAND

CAROLINE HARRISON

GLADYS ARJETTA MAYS

VIVIAN ELIZABETH MAYS

LUCIAN HENRY SHRADER

OFFICERS

VIVIAN ELIZABETH MAYS, PRES.

THEODORE HUBBARD EVANS, VICE PRES.

ARABELL MOON FALCONER, SEC. AND TREAS.

MOTTO:
"PALMO NON SINE PULVERE"

COLORS:
BLACK AND GOLD

CLASS FLOWER
DAISY

Amherst High School class of 1915 graduation program,
listing students and class officers.
Courtesy of Thurman Davis

Students at an early Amherst school.
Amherst County Historical Museum photo

If you needed a bantam rooster in Amherst during the early 1960s, all you had to do was get in touch with Johnny Wimer or Donnie Woodson.

Well, sort of.

Word got around that Allen Campbell, who at the time taught physical education and coached football, basketball and baseball at Amherst County High School, wanted a bantam rooster for his small flock of hens. Johnny and Donnie, neighbors on Old Stage Road, heard about the coach's need during a gym class one day and figured it would not hurt their standing with him at the school to try to accommodate Mr. Campbell in his quest to fill out the flock in his hen house.

It just so happened that a neighbor of the boys had a rooster and they knew where it spent its evenings. In fact, Gertrude Prior, who will always be remembered for her work on behalf of animals for the Humane Society of Amherst County, had two roosters, one of whom went by the name of Fred. They were pets of hers and ran around the yard and roosted in the trees.

But they had an annoying habit of beginning their day crowing and making a ruckus much earlier than Johnny was accustomed to rising. So he was looking forward to capturing the noisy birds and getting them out of the neighborhood.

Here's how Johnny put it: "We knew where they roosted down by her garden and went down there after dark one night and took a burlap sack, caught the two roosters, put them in the sack and took them up to a little shed behind our house."

"We carried them over to

Mr. Campbell's house the next morning, a Saturday morning, and gave them to him. Oh, he was tickled to death to have the roosters."

Johnny pointed out that Mr. Campbell lived near the Sweet Briar dairy at the time, near the Sweet Briar College campus. As it turns out, Miss Prior worked at the Sweet Briar Book Store. "Talk got around the Sweet Briar campus that Mr. Campbell had just acquired two banty roosters," Johnny said. "Well, Gert found out about it and she went to him and wanted to know if she could come see the banty roosters. So she went to his house and called Fred by name. Sure enough, there was old Fred, who responded to her call. Then she asked Mr. Campbell how he got the roosters. He told her that Donnie Woodson and Johnny Wimer had given them to him."

As Johnny tells the story, she told the unsuspecting coach and physical education teacher, "They are my roosters and I want them back. They came down there and stole them."

"We got confronted by Gert and Mr. Campbell and had to admit that we had gone down there and kidnapped the roosters and had to give them back."

So were either of the culprits, who were simply trying to make their way through high school, punished for the theft? Johnny put it this way and he's certain Donnie would agree: "We had to give the roosters back to Gert. That was punishment enough."

And Mr. Campbell, who is now retired and living in Amherst, had to look elsewhere for a rooster to complete his flock in the hen house.

– Robert Wimer

43

(Top) Amherst Training School student council members, 1956. Front, from
left: Ann Mitchell, Ernestine Davis, Jean Higginbotham, Bessie Ross, unidentified, Maurice Moore, sponsor. Back,
from left: Carroll Sandidge, Barbara Hutcherson, Miss Fletcher, Forrest Williams, Eddie Fletcher.

(Bottom) 1956 Amherst Training School French Club. Front, from left: Unidentified, Dorothy Mosby , Barbara Smith,
Naomi Reid, Ernestine Sandidge, unidentified, Gloria Higginbotham. Back, from left: Carl Williams, Ora Henley, Janette
Dempsey, Helen Williams, unidentified.
Photos from 1956 *Trojan*

AMHERST TRAINING SCHOOL OFFERED FIRM FOUNDATION

By Jean Higginbotham and Lynn Kable

Amherst Training School (ATS), originally called the Amherst Negro School, was the first high school for black students in Amherst County. It was built on School Street with black community contributions in about 1921. ATS educated students in grades one through eleven, from the northern half of Amherst County. Amherst County Public Schools added twelfth grade in 1956, and kindergarten in the 1970s. Madison Heights had no black high school until 1939. Small elementary schools fed into ATS for high school.

Amherst County public schools added the twelfth grade in 1956. ATS's high school was replaced by Central High School, another black school, in September 1956. ATS remained open until construction of the all-black Central Elementary School in 1964.

A 1941 Engineers' Report featured a school photo and description: "Amherst Negro School, Amherst, Virginia. A one-story and part basement, frame building with composition shingle roof and wood floors. Wood sealed finish, electric lighting, stove heat. Approximately 19 years old, in fair condition. Occupancy—six class rooms and kitchen."

Two additional buildings, still standing, were added. A wooden structure contained a kitchen and lunchroom. The other (now WAMV Radio) was a two-classroom brick building. Former student Willie Diggs recalled that while supposedly in bed with whooping cough, he snuck out to help dig the foundation for the brick building. Classroom coal stoves heated the main building —Mr. Diggs said his grandchildren just didn't believe it when he told them they are lucky not to have to shovel coal in school!

Students brought their lunches in the early days, but after the lunchroom was built in the 1930s, it was possible to buy lunch. Students who helped cook received free lunch and also learned cooking skills. Patricia Rose remembers "watching the hands" of the cook, Miss Jackson.

The principal from 1948 to 1956 was Nathaniel Anderson, who also conducted music programs. He held a Ph.D. and honorary degrees. "I remember him securing scholarships from colleges all over the eastern United States for graduating seniors," says Jean Higginbotham.

Edith Jones, now 102 and living in Monroe, taught first and second grade in the 1950s. Asked what she liked best about the school, Mrs. Jones stated, "The children, I just loved the children!" The feeling was mutual for many students. Gilbert Rose described Mrs. Jones as "A real nice lady—the same as a mother to me." Robert Sandidge said his favorite teacher was, "Cousin Edith!"

After graduating from Virginia State University (VSU), Annie Chambers (now Mrs. Pinn), taught government and senior English at ATS from 1948 to 50, then left for graduate school. Mrs. Pinn chuckled when she recalled that because the University of Virginia would not allow black students in their graduate guidance programs, the Commonwealth of Virginia's "Separate but Equal" requirements paid for her to obtain two master's degrees from prestigious Columbia University Teachers' College in New York.

ATS had a number of distinguished alumni. Willard Douglas Jr., class of 1949, was the first African American full-time judge in the Commonwealth of Virginia. Rev. Margaret Nelson, now pastor of St. Peter's Church in Clifford, served as a nurse and nursing instructor in the Air Force, and was the first female black colonel in that area of service.

Former ATS students have made important contributions to Amherst life: ordained minister Jasper "Eddie" Fletcher, also a Town of Amherst Magistrate; Gilbert and Patricia Rose, owners of What a Blessing Bakery; Mabel Hughes, a county school bus driver; Robert Sandidge, landscaper; Helen Williams, administrative assistant of Virginia Tech/Cooperative Extension Service with more than fifty years of service; Jean Higginbotham, a retired Amherst County social work supervisor; Gloria

LULA CARPENTER
"Lulu"
Ambition - To become a nurse.
"To win this fight, we must never surrender."

HARRY CABELL
"Shorty"
Ambition - To become a barber.
"If at first you don't succeed try, try again."

ALVIN THOMAS
"Al"
Ambition - To become a lawyer.
"Experience is the best teacher."

MARY J. SMITH
"Little One"
Ambition - To become a secretary.
"I'll study and get ready, then maybe the chance will come."

Higginbotham, a development officer at Sweet Briar; and Barbara Parks, retired teacher.

Judge Douglas remembers young black teachers, recent college graduates, as "excellent examples who showed students they could become teachers and professionals in other fields." Pastor Nelson remembers that Miss Frances Cash, Miss Annie Chambers and Miss Louise Coles were particularly dedicated, talented young teachers. Pastor Nelson credited Miss Coles, a college math major herself, with having prepared her particularly well for college mathematics by giving her extra work in geometry.

Pastor Nelson, who majored in biology at VSU, felt that ATS was poor in science: "We had very little equipment. I wondered why they let me major in biology in college when I did not have the background." When asked how she made up ground in college and nursing school science courses, Pastor Nelson said, "Hard work."

Eddie Fletcher greatly respected biology and chemistry teacher Maurice Moore: "He was a local Amherst County man. He returned to

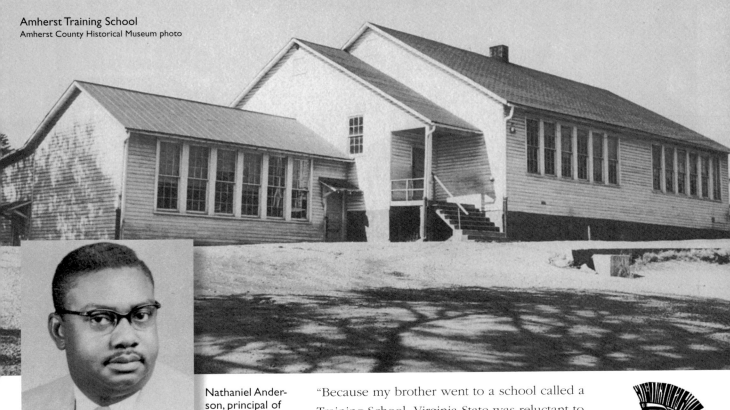

Amherst Training School
Amherst County Historical Museum photo

Nathaniel Anderson, principal of Amherst Training School, 1956.
1956 *Trojan* photo

Amherst as a teacher, having been in the service and then through college, when he was in his late 20s. The way he carried himself and conducted his life was a wonderful example for young men. He taught us that if we prepared ourselves there was no limit to where we could go in life. He was thorough in his teaching—we didn't have the science equipment in the Amherst Training School, but he was able to give us a thorough feel for the subject."

Patricia Rose recalled with joy learning about poetry at Amherst Training School. "It's something I still love today—poetry!" said Mrs. Rose.

Looking back on ATS brought a variety of reactions. Students who went on to advanced education often were asked whether they had attended an academic or trade school, because of the name "Amherst Training School." Robert Sandidge said, "It sounded like we could only be trained, not educated." Eddie Fletcher recalls,

"Because my brother went to a school called a Training School, Virginia State was reluctant to let him go into the fields he wanted to study. He had to pass an entrance exam to qualify."

Pastor Nelson remembered a feeling of community at ATS: "We were a close-knit class. Many of us remain close."

Mabel Hughes was a student in the segregated ATS, then a parent during early integration. Her own children had to pass tests in Richmond to prove they were "qualified" to attend previously all-white schools in Amherst County. Mrs. Hughes says, "I tell students on my bus that they should take advantage of all the possibilities they have in school. They have so many more opportunities than we did." ☞

Information for this article was researched and interviews conducted by Amherst Glebe Arts Response, Inc. (AGAR) for its "Three Amherst Schools" project, funded in part by a grant from the Virginia Foundation for the Humanities. Interviewers were Jean Higginbotham, Mia Magruder, Ruthie Ellenson and Lynn Kable.

FROM BASKETBALL
ON A DIRT COURT
TO DANCING ON A SLANTED FLOOR

By Leah Settle Gibbs

"Extracurriculars" can take on multiple connotations—anything from a kids' snowball fight as they walked to school to a chaperoned trip to New York.

Every Amherst mother's laundry day nightmare was red clay, with a good supply being brought home from the school playground. The rough and tumble of life during "recess" (with strong emphasis on the first syllable) accounted for an accumulation of red dirt and scraped knees and elbows.

By the 1950s, the Amherst school yard had a kid-powered merry-go-'round, a set of swings and jungle gym. Other activities during recess were largely student-devised, with a modicum of supervision.

The layout of the grounds accommodated various endeavors, with the "big kids," usually boys, engaging in baseball games on the lower field which had a screen backstop. They brought their own gloves and a couple of bats and balls were stuffed into a classroom closet. They chose up sides and played, congenially enough, figuring out the rules and strategy mostly without adult direction.

A dirt basketball court was located at the other end of the field, although baseball was the game of choice for most. Classrooms had a couple of inflated balls that could be used for dodgeball or kickball. A few girls would gather on the front sidewalk and draw a hopscotch diagram with chalk, while some of the boys were nearby, having made a circle in the dirt for shooting marbles. A larger group sometimes played "Red Rover."

Large trees with big exposed roots on the far end of the school yard set the stage for a terrestrial playhouse for young girls. More adventuresome students wandered about the school property, sometimes encircling the athletic field's perimeter of trees, weeds, and scrubby undergrowth, although it was probably off limits. This area had a well-worn path and was part of what

Amherst residents who went on to play college basketball are on their respective college's all-time scoring lists: **Terry Tabb** (5th at Lynchburg College), **Wayne Davis** (3rd at Lynchburg College), and **David Smith** (8th at Radford University).

48

was universally called "the monkey jungle."

One of the teachers would ring a hand bell to signal the end of recess, prompting disappointment and a mad dash from all parts of the school grounds.

Occasionally, the PTA would promote cultural events: a play by the Barter Theatre touring group or a visit by the artmobile of the Virginia Museum. In the 1940s, a movie would sometimes be shown in the auditorium. Ben Smith clearly remembers seeing "Last of the Mohicans."

Regular assembly programs were scheduled, with monthly chapel services led by a local minister. Student participation was encouraged with plays and spelling bees.

In the late 1950s, Methodist minister Byron Halstead volunteered his time to lead those who wished to perform in a Glee Club. This group of elementary students sang such favorites as "Bicycle Built for Two," "Erie Canal," and "Rock of Ages." In fact, the group went to Lynchburg one Saturday to record for radio station WWOD, hence affording these elementary students their 15 minutes of fame early in life.

The Virginia Cooperative Extension sponsored 4-H clubs and meetings became part of the elementary school program. Some members then pursued their projects which extended beyond the classroom with additional training and fun, first at the "short courses" at Sweet Briar, and later at Holliday Lake 4-H camp, which opened in 1941.

The Forest Service generally sent a representative to some of the elementary school classes annually for a fire safety presentation. That visit was always good for some new Smokey Bear book covers and other items, such as rulers and pencils.

Interscholastic sports were loosely organized in the early years. Baseball was probably the first such sport for boys. Boys and girls had basketball teams that used the dirt court located below the shop.

Players from the '30s remember having not enough basketball shoes for all the players, so when a substitute was sent into the action, the players switched shoes so that everybody on the court could have athletic shoes.

Not too far removed from the "peach basket" era, girls' basketball in the 1930s was a stationary game, with the court divided into three parts. A team had two forwards who were offensive players, two guards who were defensive players, and two middle-of-the-court players, called center and side-center. The center was generally the tallest one, who jumped for the ball each quarter. Their role was to relay the ball upcourt.

Heated rivalries developed with Lovingston, Temperance, and Madison Heights. One competitor recalled with disgust, "Temperance always beat the hell out of us!"

Interscholastic football was in its infancy in the early 1940s, starting initially with a form of "flag football," using a handkerchief in the back pocket for the flag. A defensive player's snatching the ball-carrier's flag was the equivalent of tackling him. Girls became cheerleaders, having no official uniforms, but exhibiting enthusiasm for the team.

By the 1950s, cheerleaders had uniforms, with monogram sweaters and full skirts.

Lucile Ware, holding basketball, with her Amherst School teammates in 1922.
Patty Turpin photo

Maggie McDearmon as a senior at Randolph-Macon College was named Old Dominion Athletic Conference Player of the Year in volleyball in 2007.

Volleyball was played as an indoor activity, even with the unique feature of the playing area at the back of the Amherst High School auditorium—a slanted floor. Whoever was on the upper side of the floor had a decided advantage. Vance Wilkins recalls spirited games, and sometimes male teachers or the principal, Jake Stone, would join the fun. Students were motivated to take advantage of their match-ups against the faculty within the fullest extent of the rules, targeting them with their spikes.

In the early '50s, the FFA entered a volleyball team in competition with other schools and

Right: Amherst High School girls' basketball team, 1931-32: Front row, from left: Helen Coleman, Evelyn Garner, Helen Rhea, Dabney Meeks, Nancy "Pete" Parr. Middle row: Bessie Watts, Maxine Chappelle, Glazier Faulkner; Back row: Bessie Lee Garbee, Eilene Canada, coach. Settle family photo

won a regional title, a significant achievement for a team that practiced on a slanted floor. That same slanted floor was the site of occasional school dances.

Helen Massie vividly remembers her senior trip in 1947. The class boarded school buses and went to Lynchburg, first to Guggenheimer's studio for a photo session, producing a composite picture of the class. This experience was followed by an afternoon at the bowling alley.

Other school trips became a much anticipated feature in the post-war years. First graders enjoyed a train ride, Amherst to Monroe. Other local destinations for walking trips were the publishing company and fire department to see how all their equipment worked. Fourth to seventh grades featured trips to Virginia his-

toric sites: Monticello, Natural Bridge, one of the Virginia caverns, and finally to Richmond (which included not only Jefferson's Capitol, but also one of Virginia's primary economic resources, a cigarette factory).

Also in the '50s, a tradition began with the senior class mounting a fund-raising effort to help finance a three-day trip to New York City. This practice was carried over to the new high school and continued into the 1970s. Seniors from those eras can still recall the details: an all-night bus ride, a city tour including the Statue of Liberty, a Broadway play, the Rockettes at Radio City, shopping, and a choice between the Ringling Brothers Circus and a professional baseball game. The crowning event was dinner at Mama Leone's, and then the all-night bus ride home, after two nights in a New York hotel.

In the 1970s, the new Amherst Elementary School was built on North Main Street. The old school building served various functions for several years, but its end had finally come, after seven decades of use. The contract for its demolition was awarded to Vance Wilkins Jr. Soon thereafter, Vance saw Mr. Stone, his former principal and volleyball opponent on that slanted floor in the auditorium, and told him that his business was going to tear down the school. Mr. Stone responded wryly, "I thought you did a pretty good job of that when you were there!" ∞

MODEST BEGINNINGS FOR HIGH SCHOOL FOOTBALL

By Leah Settle Gibbs

Hopes of another trip to the Virginia High School League football playoffs—it's almost becoming a predictable event. Success has come in recent years to Amherst County High School's team, the Lancers, but their spiritual ancestors were a small football team formed in 1944. For thirteen years, the AHS pigskin squad represented the town of Amherst before school consolidation.

Scholastic sports were minimal in that era, anyway, with considerable cutting back on many activities during wartime. For a brief period in the early '40s, Amherst had played a few games of "flag football," using a handkerchief in a hip pocket as the "flag" to be pulled out in place of tackling the ball-carrier; players recalled this type of game against teams from Rustburg and Volens. However, with the encouragement of several teachers and Jake Stone, principal and coach, Amherst High School fielded its first tackle football team that fall, playing a two-game schedule.

When the idea of forming a team was introduced, a group of boys was enthusiastic but lacking in knowledge of the game. Many had never even seen a football game. Several of them caught the bus from Amherst to Lynchburg on a couple of Saturdays that fall of 1944, changing city buses in downtown Lynchburg, proceeding to City Stadium and observing the E. C. Glass team at work. Glass at that time was among the largest high schools in Virginia and had evolved into a state powerhouse, traveling statewide to play teams from other city high schools in Richmond and Tidewater: Maury, Granby, Hampton, Thomas Jefferson, and John Marshall.

The Amherst team first scrimmaged youth teams from Lynchburg, playing a team at the Ruffner School playground and later a team from the Presbyterian Home (who had gained fame as "the shoeless wonders," a highly successful team in the city youth leagues from the 1920s to 1950s).

Russell Henderson was drafted by the Baltimore Colts in 1978 after a record-setting career as a punter at the University of Virginia. He also had tryouts with other NFL teams the following year.

51

Blackstone High School Athletic Association
BASE BALL SEASON. 1917.
BLACKSTONE, VA.
April 5, 1917.

Mr. H.Y.Watts,
Mgr. H.S.Baseball Team
Amherst, Va.

Dear Sir;-

Can you give us a game up there on April 23 with a guaran[tee] of twenty-five dollars and entertainment for thirteen men? We have a trip up the road and would be able to stop over to play you for that [am]ount. We play Appomattox and Farmville and would like to arrange anoth[er] game on that trip. Please let me hear from you as soon as possible.

Wishing you a prosperous season and hoping to receive a favorable reply soon, I remain,

Yours truly, Mgr.

The first ever game for Amherst High School was played on Friday, November 17, 1944, against Holy Cross High School from Lynchburg. The inexperienced Amherst team suffered a 39-0 loss. They acquitted themselves well in the first half, being down only 6-0 at halftime, having been thwarted only a couple of yards short of a touchdown following an interception by Vic Hanger.

Cheerleaders, wearing their typical "school clothes," chanted from the sidelines:

2-4-6-8

Who do we ap-pre-ci-ate . . .

The school newspaper account records that Holy Cross had been penalized 60 yards in the game, while Amherst had no penalties. It was also noted that quarterback "Bozie" Whitehead, a local resident who had previously attended VES and had played a little football, was injured in the

fourth quarter and had to be carried from the field.

In its second and final game of the inaugural season, Amherst lost to Randolph-Henry High School from Charlotte Courthouse. The opponent scored its 20 points in the first half, with Amherst coming out after halftime with renewed vigor, scoring 14 points. The first touchdown in Amherst football history was scored by Ben Smith on a pass from George Calkins.

The school paper, *The Blue Ranger*, noted that the Amherst team was a spirited group that second half. As a sign of the times, the newspaper article concluded:

It was a good thing for Randolph-Henry that the game was over when it was or they would have returned home with a loss, as sure as Hitler is going to lose this war.

Members of that first Amherst football team were: Dan Burley, George Calkins, Spencer Campbell, Pat Drummond, Billy Edgemon, Harry Faulconer, Jack Faulconer, Maurice "Ace" Gannaway, Mallory Hancock, Vic Hanger, Frank Hudson, Lewis Jennings, Lewis Jones, Sam Massie, Will Mays, Dick Proffitt, Bruce Ross, Earl "Mutt" Shrader, Ben Smith, Thomas "Bozie" Whitehead, Hugh Edward Woodson.

In the early years of Amherst High School football, they used whatever conditions and guile they could muster to their advantage. The field had two distinguishing features: a rough surface that was made worse by the addition of cinders and other debris from the school furnace, supplied regularly by custodian Raleigh Davis, and the brittle stubble of ragweed that

George Steinbrenner, fiery owner of the New York Yankees, had a daughter who attended Sweet Briar College in the 1970s.

had been mowed from the far side of the field. Being tackled in either of these areas meant that the players had not only been stopped, but also abraded by the elements of the surface. Amherst's strategy was designed to exploit both of these features.

The team had canvassed the town's businesses and private citizens for financial backing for their equipment, which consisted of leather helmets with no face guard and uniform shirts and pants with only the most basic padding, with maroon and gray used as team colors. Transportation to scrimmages and games was provided by the coaches' cars, with some of the team also riding in the back of somebody's pick-up truck.

With most of the team's equipment, financial needs and transportation being provided by the town's businesses and private citizens, the school newspaper expressed gratitude: "We wish to thank the good citizens of Amherst for making it possible for us to have a football team this year. None of the boys will forget the enjoyment provided for them." From a two-game, two-loss schedule and two touchdowns, a state power in high school football would eventually emerge some sixty years later. ∾

...TED BY HOLY CROSS

BOOK WEEK

Centered around the theme, "Unite Through Books," Book Week was observed November 12 through November 18 throughout the United States and in many other parts of the world.

Mrs. Lamanna, the Amherst librarian, had the library arranged with a Book Week theme. The students enjoyed visiting the library to see how "books could unite."

A chapel program was arranged for this occasion also. Mary H. Joyner spoke on "The Value of Books to Us." Sarah Gay gave a brief review of the new books in the library and also gave us helpful information about the authors of these books.

This year's Book Week play is regarded as very appropriate and plans are in progress to unite all peoples of the world.

The year of 1944 marks the 200th anniversary of the publication of the first volume for children. Is an English edition published by John Newberry in June, 1744, and is called "A Little Pretty Pocketbook."

The first American edition was published by Isiah Thomas in Massachusetts in 1787.

Book Week was originated in 1919 by Franklin Mathews, chief scout librarian. Mr. Mtahiews developed a national campaign to arouse the public interest in more and better books for children.

FIRST FOOTBALL GAME OF SEASON

Amherst, Friday, Nov. 17, in the first game of the season and first in Amherst High School history, lost to the Holy Cross Gaels 39 to 0.

The inexperienced Amherst boys allowed their opponents only six points during the first half. Hanger intercepted a Holy Cross pass in the first quarter and was tackled within only a few yards of the goal line, but Amherst was unable to score.

Things started moving for Holy Cross in the second half and by the end of the half they had accounted for five touchdowns. The Gaels were penalized sixty yards, while Amherst was not penalized at all. Whitehead was injured with four and a half minutes to play and had to be carried off the field.

POS.	HOLY CROSS	AMHERST
LE—Russel		Campbell
LT—Jordan		Woodson
LG—Padgett		Mays
C—Bowles	Dan	Burley
RT—Reinburg	Vic	Hanger
RG—		Ross
RE—Peters		Hudson
QB—Williams	Bozie	Whitehead
RH—Bragrassa		Hancock
LH—Beaton	Ben	Smith
FB—Fo drderstcfAmh shrdl etaois		
FB—Ford	John Wesley	Shrader
Holy Cross	6 0 13 20—39	
Amherst	0 0 0 0—0	

Touchdowns: Ford 3, Russel, Williams, Ray. Substitutes: Holy Cross: Mosby, Conway, Viar, Holloran, Ryan. Amherst: Edgemon.

CLASS NEWS

Clipping from the *Blue Ranger*, Amherst High School monthly newspaper.
Courtesy of Ben Smith

Martinsville Team Loses to Amherst High, 12 to 11

Amherst, April 15.—By staging a tenth inning batting rally and overcoming a three run lead Amherst high school won today from Martinsville high school by a score of 12 to 11. J. Pettyjohn who was on the mound for Amherst held the visitors to seven scattred hits but he had poor support. Errors by Gooch proved costly in the early part of the game.

Williams and Jones led the Amherst batters and Moore of Martinsville, secured four hits in five trips to the plate, and the fielding of English at

short for the visitors was little than of brilliant. Morriss, who followed Hodnett in the box with the bases full, pitched himself out of a hole.

Score by innings: R. H. E.
Amherst ... 002 131 010 4—12 13 9
Martinsville 140 001 110 3—11 7 5
Batteries: Amherst, J. Pettyjohn and Jones; Martinsville, Hodnett, Morriss and Moore. Umpires, Harrison and Blanks.

From the earliest years of the century, the crack of the bat and the yells of the fans resonated over many a countryside baseball diamond. The sport's 19th century origins had thrust it into national attention in the post-Civil War era, with teams being assembled in even the smallest towns and rural areas.

Fourth of July celebrations and fairs included ball games, commencing at dawn and running almost continually until sundown. The American Legion provided a field, complete with wooden grandstand.

A field on the Thomas Hughes property east of town was also in frequent use on weekends with teams coming from neighboring communities to compete. Baseball has long been a staple of Amherst sports, as its popularity and success countywide have produced the consistently high-ranking team at the county high school, with several players with Amherst roots ultimately making it to the major leagues.

One Amherst High School baseball game from May 1945 has become legendary. Lovingston High School, a traditional rival, boasted an especially good team that year, enjoying large margins of victory.

Amherst had lost the initial meeting by a score of 27-3. The team's missing ingredient was a dominating pitcher, and the most effective person for that role was no longer in school that spring. Regulations regarding player eligibility were a couple of decades away, so the idea that this player could play for Amherst was implemented.

The resulting 2-0 win by Amherst became the sole blemish on the Lovingston High School baseball team's record that year. This event is still discussed at social gatherings involving people from both sides of the Tye River, with differing perspectives on the legitimacy of that win—with the relative joy or vehemence in the recollection being in direct correlation to the beverages consumed. One person who was both teacher and coach commented, "Some people thought I was a crook for finagling him back into school." The heroic pitcher went on to a short career in professional baseball and the others involved have rehashed the game for 65 years.

Beyond this victory, recollections from the 1940s cite other noteworthy teams and individuals. One of the best baseball players to come from the town of Amherst was Sammy Ellington, a good student who lived near the courthouse and attended the University of Virginia, where he played a starring role and was captain of the team his final year. He passed up an early chance at professional baseball to attend college instead.

One Amherst team was especially skilled and the Amherst coach, Bill Dudley, agriculture teacher, used his connections to arrange an exhibition game in Blacksburg against the VPI freshmen. Amherst lost, but Sammy Ellington reportedly collected on a 25-cent wager for hitting a home run, much to the delight of the small Amherst cheering section.

—*Leah Settle Gibbs*

Jackie Jensen

OUTFIELD   BOSTON RED SOX

Courtesy of H.L. Hansberry III

Jackie Jensen was the only athlete to play in both the Rose Bowl and in a World Series. He was an All-American in both baseball and football while attending the University of California-Berkley and is in the College Football Hall of Fame. He played on a College World Series championship team. He was elected Most Valuable Player of the American League in 1958. Jensen, whose wife is from Amherst County, is buried in the Amherst Cemetery.

TO PLAY AMHERST HIGH

Hilltop Baseball Team to Open Season at Fair Grounds Thursday Afternoon.

The Lynchburg high school will open its season at the fair grounds Thursday afternoon when they meet the Amherst high school nine.

The Hilltoppers have a strong team this year, with six letter men back and expect little trouble in defeating the county boys although the showing made by the Amherst team thus far during the season would ...

good exhib...

Both clippings from *The News*, 1917
Courtesy of Thurman Davis

GAS LAMPS ILLUMINATED CHRISTMAS PERFORMANCE

By Lynn Kable

Students who attended all-black Amherst Training School participated in a number of programs in the community outside of school hours. While some of these activities were sponsored by the school system itself, others were community-based activities or work-based endeavors.

Willie Diggs, who attended the school in the 1930s and '40s took pleasure in special nighttime holiday performances that students put on at the school for their parents, relatives and neighbors. He said, "A highlight of the year was the Christmas performance. Norvell Blair was a local barber who also drove the school bus. Mr. Blair used to bring two gas lamps to the school every year to light the stage for the Christmas performance," Mr. Diggs recalled with a laugh. "We really enjoyed it—it was something to look forward to —something we really enjoyed doing."

Mr. Diggs said performances took place "in the evening, 7 o'clock or thereabouts. Everybody would come out. Believe it or not, hard as it was, it was beautiful—it was fantastic. Everyone came out to see their kids perform."

Several of those interviewed credited the principal from 1948 to 1956, Nathaniel Anderson, for his strong interest and talent in the field of music, and praised what he was able to do for students in that field.

Jean Higginbotham reminisced: "We had an outstanding chorus under his direction, and he brought out a well-known Lynchburg pianist, Miss Anita Jones, to accompany rehearsals and performances. We did performances at Mount Olive Church, where there was lots of seating and the acoustics were very good. We even gave a singing performance once in a nearby prison."

Mrs. Higginbotham, who attended ATS up to eighth grade in the 1950s, remembered the May Day activities including ATS students, separate for white and black students. "Activities were held on a Saturday at the fairgrounds at the end of Mount Olive Road. There were May Day dances, and each class made its own different costumes for dances around a maypole. The extension office sponsored homemaker exhibitions of home canned goods, and sewn and knitted garments, with prizes awarded for the best work."

Pastor Margaret Nelson, class of 1950, experienced a summer work and travel opportunity that was available for sixteen- to eighteen-year-old students: "We went up to Connecticut to work during the summers in tobacco. Boys were pulling the leaves off the plants, delivering them to the girls. Girls were scoring tobacco on sticks. Cooks from the school went up with the students when they went to work. It paid enough to get you some clothes when you got back. Our group even gave a concert on the

Amherst Training School cheer-leaders, 1956
From The 1956 *Trojan*

tobacco farm." Pastor Nelson said she liked participating in this work program because it gave students a chance to travel outside Central Virginia.

Mrs. Higginbotham remembered from the mid-1950s, "The first year I went to the tobacco fields I cut my hands to shreds using string to tie the tobacco to overhead hanging racks. Then, we spent the summer sewing leaves together to be hung and cured. The next two

years I worked in the kitchen, which was less labor intensive but you had to rise at 4:30 a.m. to cook breakfast."

Sports were an area in which many students wanted to participate but the opportunity did not exist at Amherst Training School, where there was no gym, and only a small play yard. Recreational space and equipment for ATS students consisted of a dirt ball field in the back of the school, an old swing set, several types of balls, and a basketball hoop.

Judge Willard Douglas Jr., who graduated in 1949, told of participating in an all-black baseball league sponsored by the community. They were called the Royal Dukes, and they played out past Smitty's Restaurant on Route 60, on land they purchased for a baseball field. The Royal Dukes traveled to Nelson County and Buckingham to play league games. "We all piled in the same car," Judge Douglas recalled.

Duvall Sandidge remembered that Amherst Training School was able to use Gordon's Fairgrounds for an occasional baseball game in the mid-1950s. In 1956, the last year that ATS had a high school, a baseball team that was going to play in Nelson County was in a head-on collision on top of Buffalo hill, and three members of the team were severely injured. The rest of the baseball season was cancelled.

Eddie Fletcher (ATS student in the mid-'50s) said, "We played basketball and sandlot football because we didn't have a real field, or helmets. We were lucky to get a ball. I feel that I could have excelled in a sports field if I had had the opportunity to learn as a youngster, rather than trying to pick it all up after I was grown. It would have been nice if we could have also learned skills in communications, mechanical work, or agriculture. We didn't have those choices."

Pastor Nelson said that although there was a basketball hoop out in the play yard by the school, "We never saw a basketball or football

PERCY HIGGINBOTHAM

Craftsman. Self-taught woodworker. Carpenter. Painter. Keen businessman. Sunday School teacher. Such were the terms used to describe Percy Higginbotham, the man to whom everybody in Amherst turned for building expertise.

Higginbotham's first work experiences were with the railroad, employment that left him blind in one eye. He operated a funeral home that later became Wright's Funeral Home. His woodworking and painting skills then provided his full-time occupation for the rest of his life.

Higginbotham worked as a young man with other carpenters, learning the trade by the hands-on method, but beyond that, was self-taught, as evidenced by his extensive collection of woodworking books found among his possessions. Many structures in town still stand as a testament to his skills practiced in mid-century.

Not only did he work for people all around town, but he also constructed his own home, adding to it as his income would allow. He also built various accessories for his home, such as Adirondack chairs and a children's swing.

Many remember his long-standing habit of teaching Sunday school at Mt. Olive, where he was superintendent of the Sunday school for thirty years, then walking to Union Hill Baptist Church, east of town, where he also maintained membership and served as deacon.

His civic involvements included the zoning board, the Christian Aid Society, NAACP, and PTA.

James Lee Higginbotham enjoys the swing made by his grandfather, Percy Higginbotham. The elder Higginbotham also crafted the Adirondack chairs in the back yard.
Jean Higginbotham photo

game until we went to college. At college we were told we had to go out and root for people. We didn't know when to root so we went out and sat behind everyone else so we could watch other people and know how and when to root."

The lack of teams and opportunities to "root" did not, however, keep the students from establishing a cheerleading squad in the 1950s. There is a picture of the cheerleaders in the 1956 year-book from Amherst Training School, *The Trojan*, in the Amherst County Historical Museum. "It was a dream," says Jean Higginbotham, "We didn't have any teams at Amherst Training School, but we had cheerleaders."

After 1956, those who went on to attend Central High School finally were able to have athletic experiences, both for playing and for cheering. ∽

The freshman class at Amherst Training School in 1956. This class became the Central High School class of 1959.
From The 1956 *Trojan*

Wedding at Mt. Olive Church in the early 1950s. Front from left, Olden Higginbotham, Bea Rose, Rebecca Higginbotham; back, bride and groom, Mr. and Mrs. James Rose Jr.
Jean Higginbotham photo

The original Emmanuel Methodist Church, which stood on East Court Street to the left of the courthouse entrance.
Amherst County Historical Museum photo

SEVERAL CONGREGATIONS PREDATE TOWN'S FOUNDING

By James D. Settle

The village of Amherst and nearby settlements have been Christian-oriented communities from their earliest days. Congregations of faith have been an integral part of Amherst's daily life, providing spiritual sustenance and opportunities for social interaction.

Documentation of founding dates of churches is sometimes difficult to confirm. Records show that groups have met in a variety of locations—the courthouse, homes, fields, schools, funeral homes, other denominations' buildings—before the actual founding of the church. Financing then often required years before the congregation could settle into permanent quarters.

Among the nine churches currently serving the town, the first to officially organize was the Presbyterian. **Amherst Presbyterian Church**, established in 1831, met at the courthouse to do so. Some of their early services were held in a nearby field, as well as other locations around the county. The Presbyterian church building, constructed in the following decades on land given by Robert Brown, was completed in 1880.

Later improvements to the property have included the addition of memorial windows, a fellowship and educational wing, and a basement under the sanctuary. The low head clearance in the basement is attributed to the fact that the basement was dug by hand, under the existing structure.

Amherst Presbyterian Church is now a member of the Presbyterian Church, USA.

Two Episcopal churches in Amherst County, St. Mark's in Clifford and St. Luke's in Pedlar Mills, preceded **Ascension Church**, the founding of which provided a more central location as the county seat grew. Construction of the church on Main Street began in 1847 on property given by Elijah Fletcher, whose land holdings later became the site of Sweet Briar College.

The name "Ascension," according to tradition, was chosen as a result of Vestryman George Christian's noticing that word on a piece of paper. Ascension Church was consecrated in 1848. At a later time, the bell tower was erected. Elijah Fletcher desired to hear the church bells at his home, three miles distant, and donated the bell for that purpose.

The parish house was completed in 1922, and

has ever since served the town for numerous community activities. Ascension Church is part of the Diocese of Southwest Virginia, with national affiliation with the Episcopal Church of the USA.

Methodist influence was probably in Amherst County by the mid-nineteenth century, with their itinerant ministers serving several congregations. During the Civil War years, the Amherst Circuit included as many as fifteen churches. The first record of the Court House Church is 1867.

Three years later, the name became Emmanuel Methodist Church, with the building on Courthouse Square remaining in use for ninety-five years, until a larger building was occupied on the north end of Main Street. Memorial stained glass windows, as well as various furnishings and accessories, were moved to the new building. The name was changed to **Emmanuel United Methodist Church** in 1968 when the Methodist Church joined with the United Brethren to form the United Methodist Church.

It was only with emancipation and the end of the Civil War that African slave descendants could officially organize religious communities and establish independent houses of worship. Earliest of those churches in Amherst was Mt. Olivet Colored Baptist Church, opened in 1876 under the leadership of the Rev. Harrison Goode. Mount Olivet not only served as a spiritual beacon to its members; the church also established the first schoolhouse for the town's Negro children. The church became a center of activities for youth, and was soon perceived as having outgrown its rather small buildings.

The congregation considered options for expansion. In 1899, after extensive deliberation, Rev. Goode and the majority of the membership relocated to West Court Street in an abandoned tobacco warehouse, which then became **Mount Olive Baptist Church**.

By mid-20th century, the church membership had grown significantly, enabling the congregation to improve the facilities with several additions and renovations.

When the Mt. Olivet congregation voted to split assets, the minority retained the original church and school. That group immediately set about the task of rebuilding their "new" church with a prayer vigil, seeking guidance in re-establishing the church's identity. Upon exiting the prayer meeting, members witnessed the rising of the morning star. With renewed spirit, they took the name **Morning Star Baptist Church**. Morning Star has enjoyed strong leadership and has continued to grow, with several renovations and improvements to its church property. Both Mt. Olive and Morning Star are affiliated with the Rockfish Baptist Association.

The influence of the Baptists has been evi-

BEN PADGETT

Ben Padgett rented a room in the backyard of the venerable 18th century Central Hotel located just across the street from what is now Travelers Restaurant. Every morning for many years during the 1920s, '30s, and '40s, he would walk down the hill to the Amherst depot and collect the town's mail. Even as an old and bent over man, he could be seen faithfully trudging up the hill with the large sack of mail on his back soon to be dropped off at the Amherst post office.

Someone asked Ben why he didn't belong to any Amherst church and he provided a quotable reply. The Baptist church was out of the question because a man who replaced him as a mail carrier belonged there. The Methodist church was suggested but that idea was scuttled because he would have to work under the postmistress who was a member there. When finally someone suggested to Ben that he become an Episcopalian, he said, "No, those people don't know when to sit down or stand up."

dent in Central Virginia since the 1700s, with Mt. Moriah and Ebenezer having been founded well before 1800. Mt. Moriah stands as the oldest church structure still in existence in the county, and Ebenezer is the oldest continuously functioning church in the county. Baptists formed **Amherst Baptist Church** in 1883, and completed their building on Second and Washington Streets in 1884.

One of the notable design features of the church was the ornate pressed tin ceiling, a touch common to the Victorian period. The church was later renovated and remodeled, with the additions for education and fellowship. After 123 years, Amherst Baptist moved to a location just west of town in 2006.

Amherst Baptist Church is affiliated with the Southern Baptist Convention.

A 20th century church serving the Amherst community is **Blue Ridge Baptist Church**. Initially called Christ Independent Church, the congregation organized in the late 1960s, meeting in a funeral home under the pastoral guidance of the Rev. Joe Thompson. The founding congregation comprised people who had become disenchanted with their former churches' wider affiliations.

Because the church membership practiced baptism by immersion, they adopted the name Christ Independent Baptist Church. A new sanctuary and activity building were completed on Blue Ridge Lane in 1970, hence the source of the current name. Blue Ridge is affiliated with the Bible Baptist Fellowship International.

The Church of the Epiphany of the Anglican Catholic Church, an outgrowth of the old Lexington parish, was established in 1976. Much of the original membership had separated from Ascension Church over differences in interpretation of doctrine and church practices. Under the leadership of the Rev. John Pedlar, they met in the old Parr Building on Second Street while formulating a plan for

Wedding of Robbie D. Mantiply and Tommy Howell, Amherst Baptist Church, 1953, before the interior was renovated. Officiant is Rev. John S. Moore.
Robbie Mantiply Howell photo

a permanent home. Their Williamsburg-style church with tower and carillon on Epiphany Court off Sunset Drive was dedicated in 1986 by The Rt. Reverend William Rutherford, Bishop of the Diocese of the Mid-Atlantic States of the Anglican Catholic Church. Local residents enjoy the carillon's hourly chimes and renditions of familiar hymns.

Holy Cross Church in Lynchburg provided Catholic Communion to twelve parishioners in Amherst on a monthly basis in the 1880s and soon helped in building a small chapel. The Church of St. Thomas the Apostle, just south of the current traffic circle, was dedicated in 1884.

Thomas Fortune Ryan of Oak Ridge in Nelson County contributed significantly to the cost of the church. The church reportedly was thriving and considering enlargement. However, the chapel ceased regular services in the 1920s.

Holy Cross Church in the 1980s introduced a Lenten Revival program in homes, with about six families. A growing congregation then acquired property on the south end of Main Street. With volunteer labor and assistance, in addition to

Left: Ascension Church, after the erection of bell tower, financed by Elijah Fletcher.
Amherst County Historical Museum photo

Kate R. Scott's drawing of Ascension Church before erection of the bell tower.
Courtesy of Helen Massie

gifts of furnishings, even stained glass windows, from other parishes, **St. Francis of Assisi Catholic Church** was dedicated in 2004. St. Francis is a member of the Catholic Diocese of Richmond of the Roman Catholic Church.

Ecumenism has been part of Amherst Christian life, with jointly operated Vacation Bible Schools, youth activities, and community Thanksgiving services. Congregations evolve and buildings are changed to accommodate projected needs, but the basic message and function of these Christian churches have remained essentially the same over parts of three centuries in Amherst. ⌒

The congregation of Amherst Baptist Church in the early 1930s.
Amherst Baptist Church photo

This sketch of "Amherst Courthouse" was drawn by Alfred Brown Petticolas in 1858. One recognizable building is Ascension Church on the left showing the original steeple.
Courtesy Virginia Historical Society

PAUL WAILES III

Paul Wailes III, whose Virginia roots run deep, is the source of much of the information gleaned for Amherst's centennial observance. His memory of people, places, events, and dates is unparalleled.

A keen interest in and pursuit of knowledge of history, coupled with the art of paying attention and remembering details, have rendered Wailes as the most knowledgeable person in town regarding who did what, when, and why. His ancestors not only played key roles in the early years of the Commonwealth but also kept documents and photographs. His lifelong residence on Garland Avenue is a veritable museum of Virginia history.

From his earliest years, he listened as his elders regaled him with tales of their youth. He remembers knowing a woman who was born 15 years before the Civil War and died at 103 in 1938.

His father's service in the Virginia Senate enabled him to gain entry into the Capitol to witness an historic event in a joint session of the legislature in 1946: addresses by Winston Churchill and Gen. Dwight Eisenhower. Churchill had delivered his famous "Iron Curtain Speech" in Missouri three days earlier.

Wailes' maternal roots in Virginia extend to the 17th century. A group comprising Peter Jefferson, William Cabell, Col. Joshua Fry, Mr. Howard for whom Howardsville is named, and Mrs. Ed Scott, Wailes' ancestor, met at the Scott home in 1744 to form the original Albemarle County. That land mass now includes Albemarle, Nelson, and Amherst counties. The town of Scottsville is named for his maternal ancestors.

Wailes continues to provide vital tidbits in the collection of Amherst history, all the while living the life of the dapper Virginia gentleman, donning dress shirt with cuff links and tie before making his daily rounds.

Paul Wailes III, right, with his parents, Paul and Hester Scott Wailes.
Paul Wailes III photo

Rob Mantiply in his grocery store at the corner
of Main and West Court streets, around 1938.
Robbie Howell photo

Goods

& Services

Alice Rucker chats with Emma and Virgil Bernard in front
of her house on Main Street in 1930.
Paul Wailes III photo

BUYING LOCALLY WAS THE NORM ON MAIN STREET

By Leah Settle Gibbs

Buy locally—hardly a modern concept.

People on foot, going from place to place to acquire goods, settle accounts, and otherwise take care of business, legal, or medical needs was a daily routine in the town of Amherst early in its first century.

At one point, several grocers were simultaneously in operation—Milton Drummond, later his son Roy; Mrs. E. M. Mays; Rob Mantiply, then his son-in-law Tommy Howell; Wade Wood, along with brother Jim; Robert Kent, and nephew William. All on Main Street, with Creed Jordan, and son Ed Lee, on Depot Street, and John Shrader, with the help of his son John Wesley, on Court Street. These stores also occasionally carried a few "notions and dry goods" in addition to groceries.

Wade Wood invested $6 and opened a store around 1900. Tommy Littrell remembers his grandfather Wood's store with the typical "pot bellied stove," penny candy counter, and shelves that ran floor to ceiling. He recalls the '48 Ford pick-up his grandfather bought for deliveries.

The customer would present the grocer with a list, either in person or by telephone. The store's employees retrieved items to be packed into a box. The customer might stop by to pick up the order, or it would be delivered to the home before dinner time. The more modern use of self-service carts became commonplace in the 1950s.

In the era of slow communication, "crepe hanging" was practiced at a post office or business. At the time of an Amherst death, the postman would receive notification, and would hang a bow of black crepe outside the post office door, with a written account of the deceased person's life, death, and funeral arrangements for all to see.

Local people would see the black crepe bow and come to read the details. By 1923, the post office had moved from the site of Joe Goodwin's store (current location of the Thrift Shop) across the street, midblock. When the post office moved again and Rob Mantiply opened a grocery store in the same location in the early 1930s, he continued the practice. Milton Drummond later opened a grocery store in the same building, and the tattered and weathered crepe bow was again placed outside the door. This practice ceased in the late 1940s.

A memorable advertising ploy was part of the Wolverine Shoe Company's efforts to show the water resistant qualities of its boots. A boot was frozen into a block of ice, with the assistance of the Wydners at the mill. The ice-encased boot then was displayed in the store window, with a contest to determine at what point the ice would melt. This gimmick drew much attention to both the product and the business, operated at that time by Milton Drummond.

Seeds, fertilizer, hardware, shoes, and coal could be acquired at Joe Goodwin's store, at the corner of Main and Second streets. His building later housed other businesses, including Grover Cleveland "Jeweler" Smith's jewelry store.

Car dealerships abounded. A series of owners operated outlets for American cars. Ford: Apperson Lee, Charles Younis, Ashby Watts, Barnes Brockman. Chevrolet: O. V. Hanger and Joe Goodwin, Webb Babcock Sr., Alfred

Mrs. E. M. Mays' grocery store on Main Street, on the site of Rucker Insurance, offered canned goods, household staples, and fresh meat, produce, and dairy products until the mid-1930s.
Paul Wailes III photo

Barrow, Joe Sullender, P. D. "Bee" Brockman. Dodge and Plymouth: Stafford Douty. Two of the Brockman sons, Kendall and Johnny, now manage the only remaining dealership for new cars in Amherst County.

Individual ownership of automobiles required support businesses: car repair, tire repair, "filling stations." A few businesses, even Shrader's grocery store, had a single gas pump outside at the street. Dayton Storey operated a car repair bay in the Goodwin building as did Ad Garland on West Court. Tires were bought, mounted, and repaired by George and J. C.

The first woman to pass Virginia's state bar examination had an Amherst connection. **Carrie Gregory** was legal assistant for many years to Jack Lee, who was Amherst County Commonwealth's Attorney from 1886 to 1894. Miss Gregory passed the bar exam in 1920.

Tastee Freez, opened in the 1960s by Donald Price and Robert "Putch" Burks.
Amherst Historical Museum photo

Gulf Station at the traffic circle, in the 1960s.
Amherst Historical Museum photo

Esso Station at the traffic circle, operated by Lawrence Massie.
Amherst Historical Museum photo

Manager of the Amherst ABC store is Pres Manuel, brother of Charlie Manuel, World Series winning manager of the Philadelphia Phillies in 2008.

Top: Georgie and Judy Staton work behind the counter at the Glendale Pharmacy in the 1960s.
Amherst County Historical Museum photo

Above: Display of merchandise at Wailes Stop-in Shop in 1965.
Paul Wailes III photo

Barbers Joe Whitten, Norvell Blair, Epoch Higginbotham, and Jim Watson kept the town's men shaved and trimmed.

Shoes were repaired by Chester Rucker from his home, after learning the trade with Clarence Camden in his shoe business on Main Street.

Paul Wailes' first venture into the retail world began on the same site in 1955, starting in sales of men's shoes and work clothing. After he married Ellen Lee the same year, she became a vital cog in the operation. Mrs. Wailes added popular lines of women's clothing, which attracted clientele throughout Central Virginia. The store changed locations twice before closing after 47 years.

The Golden Glow Dairy opened in the early 1950s. Norman Patteson and Maurice Gannaway Sr., with small dairy herds, provided milk for customers in town. They also had a small eatery featuring lunches for townspeople and snacks for school children walking home in the afternoon. Mrs. Hazel Barfield served many hot dogs, milkshakes, and ice cream cones at the Golden Glow.

Several insurance agencies served the community. One of the oldest was C. L. Scott Insurance, which Hester Scott Wailes operated for many years following her father's death. Other insurance agents in town were Ruth and Bigby Davis, Virginia Wright and Bev Harrison.

Commonly known as "The Dime Store," the Ben Franklin store provided a variety of practical items, from sewing and kitchen supplies for the home to paper, pencils, and rulers for students. Originally on the west side of Main Street, Ben Franklin moved in the early '50s next to Drummond's.

Cash or Wilson Gregory. Jeweler Smith, Frank Addison and Leslie Gregory operated car repair businesses, as well. The ever-growing popularity of the automobile slowly replaced the need for Bill Yancey's blacksmith shop on West Court Street.

A series of five druggists dealt their potions from the same location on Main Street—S. A. Day, Kearfott, Wills, Tom Hatcher, and Blair Robertson. School children stopped by the soda fountain in the Hatcher era to be introduced to a "cherry Coke" and "Nabs."

Shopping center developed by Paul Wailes, Tommy Howell, and Rex Pixley in 1960.
The News & Advance photo

WESTERN AUTO   Gift House Stamps   HOWELL'S SUPER MARKET   WAILES STOP-IN SH

EDDIE RODWELL

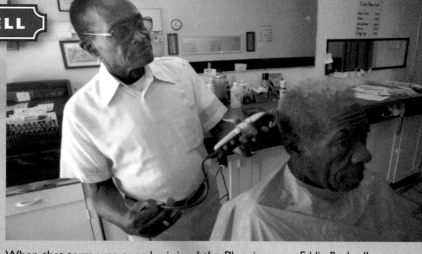

During the 1980s and 1990s, Eddie Rodwell was a presence in Amherst. He was a member of Town Council, served briefly as mayor in 1991–92, was a member of the Planning Commission and during the moments left over in his day, ran his barbershop.

Rodwell was first elected to the council in 1976 and served eight terms by the end of 1992. He achieved a racial milestone in 1991 when he was appointed by the other council members to fill the unexpired term of Mayor Joseph Siegrist. That made Rodwell the first black mayor of the town— a significant event in the town's history.

He first ran for Town Council, he told a reporter for *The News & Advance*, on a single issue: "Outhouses." He knew too many in town who didn't have indoor plumbing because they weren't connected to the town sewer system.

Referring to his election in 1976, he said he believed the time had come for a black resident to be elected to the council. But he wanted more than to be just a representative for blacks in the town. "I went into office with the idea that I was not going to represent one segment of the people. Whether they were black or white, I was going to represent all of the people."

He served five terms, was defeated in 1988 and came back for two more terms in 1990 and 1992.

When that term was over, he joined the Planning Commission where he served until his health began to deteriorate.

Rodwell's barbershop was a one-man operation, and he liked it that way. "I can just come in when I feel like it," he once said. The record shows that he usually felt like keeping the shop open and talking to his customers.

Former Amherst County Board of Supervisors' member Stanley Harris recalled that Rodwell "had a good sense of humor. He kept something going all the time."

The councilman, who fought in the Battle of the Bulge in 1944 and who retired from B&W, died in May 2005.

Eddie Rodwell with a customer in his barbershop in Amherst.
The News & Advance photo

Their array of comics, from *The Lone Ranger* to *Superman* to *Donald Duck* and *Uncle Scrooge*, as well as the more serious *Classics Illustrated* (a good resource for school reports), consumed many weekly allowances. The economic impact in the late 1950s of Dell Comics' inflation from a dime to fifteen cents, when one's allowance was a quarter, necessitated learning the concept of careful fiscal planning or creative negotiating for a raise.

Everyone eventually needs a funeral service. Washington Shrader, an early carpenter in Amherst, made coffins and opened a funeral home; his daughter Virginia married Meredith

Left:
Terry Brown, pharmacist, in front of Glendale Pharmacy.
The News & Advance photo

Drummond's grocery store and Ben Franklin, developed by the Drummonds in 1955.
The News & Advance photo

Wright, who then continued to operate the business, later with his nephew John Meredith Wright in the same position.

One of the earliest inhabitants of the area was W. W. Gilbert, whose funeral home was later operated by L. V. Parr, then by his widow Estelle Parr. Diuguid's of Lynchburg later assumed responsibility for that business. One of their employees, Dave Driskill, opened his own funeral home, now functioning under the same name with other ownership.

There was one prominent attorney who would relieve himself out of his second story office above Main Street. Most townspeople knew to walk on the other side of the street but there were rumors that a few less vigilant pedestrians got an unwelcome dousing.

Gone are the days of walking from business to business while seeing friends and neighbors. Parents no longer feel they can safely allow their children to walk home from school. With malls that house multiple stores and businesses, as well as "super centers" featuring banks, eye exams, hair cuts and tire rotation, in addition to groceries, clothing, plants, jewelry, and televisions, the business of a "town" has been transformed.

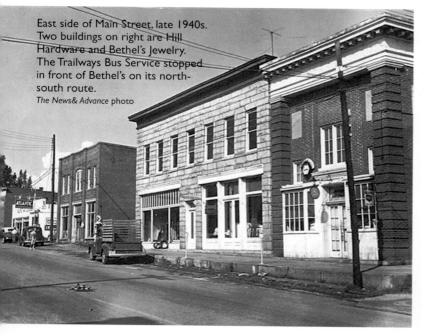

East side of Main Street, late 1940s. Two buildings on right are Hill Hardware and Bethel's Jewelry. The Trailways Bus Service stopped in front of Bethel's on its north-south route.
The News& Advance photo

Top to bottom:
School group in Farmers and Bank of Amherst.
Amherst County Historical Museum photo

Wachovia Bank on the site formerly occupied by the Robertson house.
Amherst County Historical Museum photo

"The Robertson house" was razed to accommodate the new bank building in 1963.
Amherst County Historical Museum photo

The Briar Patch Restaurant has been the location of several businesses in its time: a restaurant called "Tommie's Inn," a lawn and garden center, a shop with sewing and knitting supplies, and the Briar Patch.

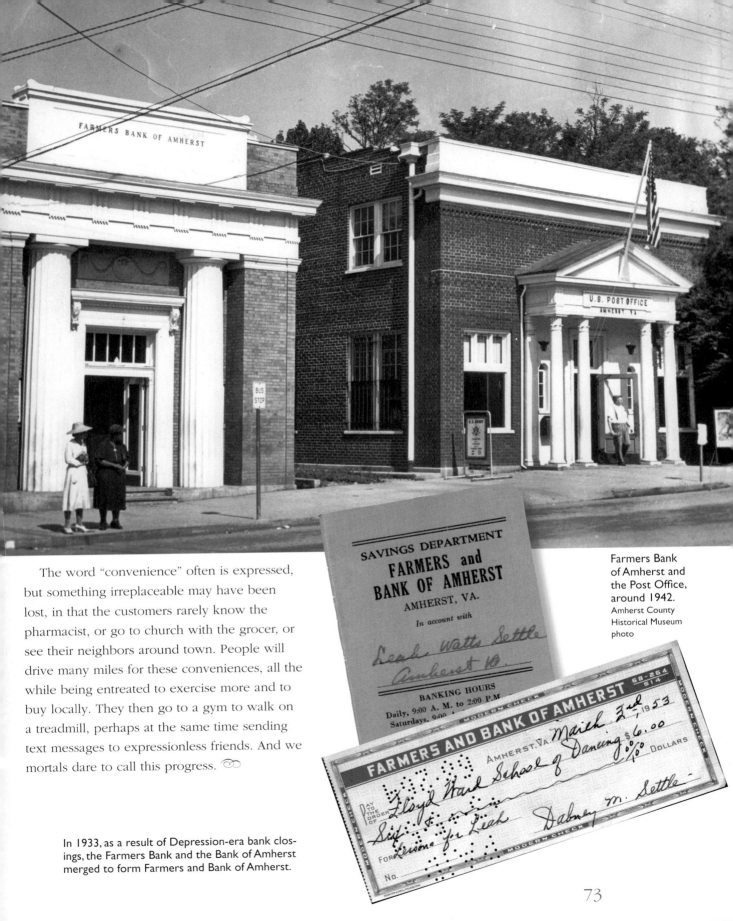

The word "convenience" often is expressed, but something irreplaceable may have been lost, in that the customers rarely know the pharmacist, or go to church with the grocer, or see their neighbors around town. People will drive many miles for these conveniences, all the while being entreated to exercise more and to buy locally. They then go to a gym to walk on a treadmill, perhaps at the same time sending text messages to expressionless friends. And we mortals dare to call this progress. ∽

In 1933, as a result of Depression-era bank closings, the Farmers Bank and the Bank of Amherst merged to form Farmers and Bank of Amherst.

Farmers Bank of Amherst and the Post Office, around 1942.
Amherst County Historical Museum photo

SAVINGS DEPARTMENT
FARMERS and
BANK OF AMHERST
AMHERST, VA.

In account with

Leah Watts Settle

Amherst V

BANKING HOURS
Daily, 9:00 A. M. to 2:00 P.M
Saturdays, 9:00

FARMERS AND BANK OF AMHERST

68-264
514

AMHERST, VA. *March 3rd* 19*53*

PAY TO THE ORDER OF *Floyd Ward School of Dancing* $ *6.00*

Six .... 00/100 DOLLARS

FOR *Lessons for Leah*   *Dabney M. Settle*

No.

Above:
Bill Wydner and
R.M. Wydner Sr.,
at the Amherst
Milling Company,
around 1995.
Amherst County
Historical Museum
photo

Right:
Workforce at
Sunnyside
Boxwood Farm
in the 1930s
Courtesy of
Susan W. Mays

FAMILY BUSINESSES ENDURE
CHANGING ECONOMIC CLIMATES

By Leah Settle Gibbs

Seven businesses in Amherst remain as multigenerational family-owned enterprises that have been in continuous operation for more than half of Amherst's first century: Hill Hardware, Sunnyside Boxwood Farm, Smitty's Restaurant, Amherst Milling Company, Burch and Ogden, Mays Farmers Service, and Sam P. Massie Insurance.

In the early 20th century, W. W. Hill founded Hill Wagon and Buggy Works, which evolved into Hill Hardware. Later partnerships developed, with multiple generations of the Turner family becoming involved, starting around 1920.

W. Wills (Billy) Turner Jr., along with his son Walter, provide contractors and the public with building and hardware supplies, as well as coal in earlier times, now heating oil. Those renovating older homes know that a needed item that might seem almost impossible to locate can often be found somewhere in Hill Hardware. A related business, Hill House, managed now by Sharon Turner, evolved from Hill Hardware in the 1980s, featuring home furnishings and accessories.

• • •

Sunnyside Boxwood Farm owes its origins to the fact that Amherst provided a rail stop when Cleveland wholesale florist Frank Williams traveled south to Florida to escape winters on Lake Erie. He often stopped in Lynchburg to pick up boxwood clippings, and a local resident suggested Central Virginia as a good retirement location. He sought a site with red clay and ideal conditions for growing American and English boxwood.

Williams acquired the property in 1928 and began Sunnyside in 1930. It has been in continuous operation since that time, with granddaughter Susan Williams Mays now the owner. Her husband, Will, is the treasurer and director, and son Frank the manager, overseeing daily operations. Boxwoods from Amherst grace such locations as the White House, the National Arboretum and gardens of the Smithsonian. The rich and famous of "The Hamptons" on Long Island maintain their privacy with the help of large American boxwoods from Sunnyside Boxwood Farm of Amherst.

The year that Route 60 opened as the east-west corridor, 1936, Thomas Hughes built a gas station, store, and restaurant at the eastern edge of the town. The establishment also featured a dance hall in the back. The name of the business later changed to Smitty's Place, operated by Thomas Hughes' sister and her husband, Ethel and David Smith. Mrs. Smith also operated a hair salon in a room above a garage on the same property.

When the Amherst bypass was being built, the configuration of the roads in that area would be changed significantly, requiring a move to another location. Smitty's Restaurant then was constructed about two miles east on Route 60, opening in 1969. Thomas Hughes' granddaughter Anita Sorrells and her daughter LaKisha continue to operate the restaurant there. Hence, Smitty's Restaurant is now only two years away from its 75th anniversary, with the fourth generation of the family operating it.

A mill at the site of Amherst Milling Company began operation in the 1700s, long before the incorporation of the town. Richard M. Wydner Sr., acquired the current mill in 1940. His son, Bill, with assistance from the next two generations, daughter Anne and her sons, maintains the gristmill along Rutledge Creek.

The variety of merchandise runs the gamut: from corn meal to chicken feed to bales of straw, from young plants to garden seeds to weed killer, from a twist of chewing tobacco to dog collars to hummingbird feeders and bluebird boxes.

Customers gather not only to fill their farming and gardening needs, but also to swap information of national or local importance, hear stories of yesteryear, or compare notes on the weather.

Gas station and restaurant built by Thomas Hughes when Route 60 was completed in the 1930s.
Anita Sorrells photo

Yale Burch and Bill Ogden in front of their appliance store in the Goodwin Building at the corner of Second and Main streets, around 1950.
Amherst County Historical Museum photo

The mill provides entertainment for children as they interact with various kinds of fowl milling about.

Historians have long appreciated the uniqueness of the mill's construction and operation. Artists find inspiration in its every angle. Where else could one buy bird seed, hear the weather report, witness a peacock's preening, and provide a critique for a local artist's latest effort?

• • •

Most Amherst homes probably had a Philco as their first TV in the 1950s. Following World War II, Yale Burch and W. A. (Bill) Ogden Sr., opened Burch & Ogden in the Goodwin building on Main Street. The company specialized in heating and plumbing, and sold and serviced Philco televisions and Maytag washers and dryers.

In the 1960s, Burch and Ogden moved across

extensive operation with farm and garden services and supplies, as well as distribution of heating oil and furnace service.

The business, with the founders' daughter Marlene Mays Fitzgerald now at the helm, bears the name Mays Farmers Service, Inc., and has divisions operating in Nelson County, Brookneal, and Lynchburg. One direct holdover from the original business remains—Stanford Harvey, now with the Nelson County operation, has been employed by the Mays family from the day the doors opened in the early 1950s.

• • •

Also in 1953, Sam Massie Sr., opened an insurance agency representing the Virginia Farm Bureau. The first office was in a small brick building just south of the town center. He moved to the current location at 165 South

the street to its current location. After a period as Burch Ogden and Schrader, the business is now owned by the Ogden family and is in its seventh decade. Under the direction of W. A. Ogden Jr., the business focuses on Maytag and Amana appliances, with sales and service, furniture, and major appliance parts.

• • •

Marshall and Arlene Mays started a farm supply business on Second Street, site of the former Amherst Livery, in 1953. In 1960, the Mays family changed location to the south side of town and began its affiliation with the Southern States franchise, leading to a more

Main Street in 1954, and changed to Nationwide Insurance beginning in 1957, when that company became an outgrowth of Virginia Farm Bureau. Massie retired in 1988 and sold the building and business to his son, Sammy Massie Jr., who continues in the same location, with his wife, Sharon.

Families who run these businesses have demonstrated the perseverance necessary to cope with changing economic times. They have adapted and remain as strong today as ever. ∞

Left: Nationwide Insurance employees, Cindy Sale and Myrna Cash, in the early 1970s. Amherst County Historical Museum photo

Above: Longtime employee Myers Campbell and Marshall Mays, right, at the Southern States Cooperative. Amherst County Historical Museum photo

The Allen Building, with the G&T Restaurant on the main floor, with the Goodwin Building behind and the Central Hotel across Second Street, around 1946.
Amherst New Era-Progress photo

A business card for the Seminole Restaurant and its cartoon flip side.

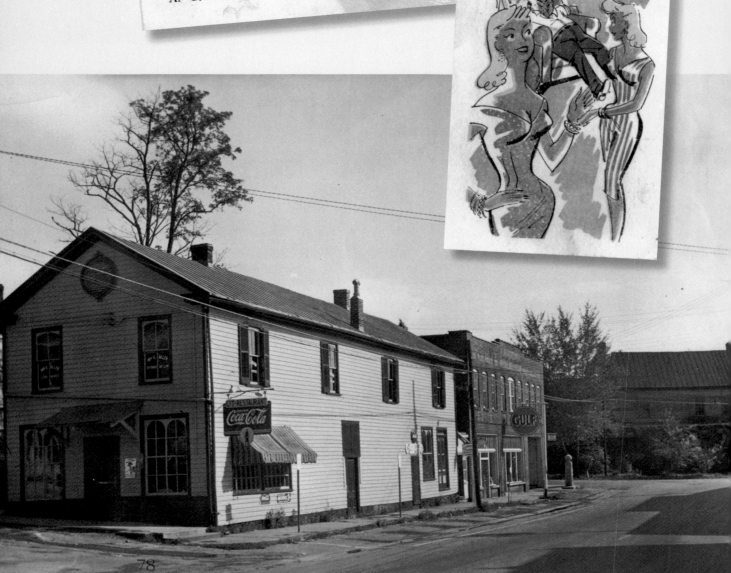

SINCE 1937   DIAL WHitehall 6-7901

Seminole Restaurant

"Those who know Eat Here"

Breakfast — Dinner — Supper

A. G. GREKOS   AMHERST, VIRGINIA

HE'S AT THE AGE WHERE HE CAN'T TAKE YES FOR AN ANSWER

A DESTINATION FOR
IMMIGRANT FAMILIES

By Leah Settle Gibbs

At first glance, the town of Amherst would appear to be ethnically and demographically the standard profile of the long-settled South: British Isles and northern European in its Caucasian population, African-American of long residence, most with English surnames, and those of Monacan Indian ancestry. But—surprisingly for a rather isolated town in the Piedmont—Amherst has attracted immigrants from not-so-traditional backgrounds.

By mid-century, Amherst had become a destination for several immigrant families who arrived for a variety of reasons. A few academicians at Sweet Briar, as well as scientists and other professionals at American Cyanamid, constituted a part of the foreign-born population. The families introduced here came to America seeking business opportunities and better lives that awaited them.

The Pfister family arrived on Ellis Island in 1906 and journeyed to Wisconsin to join other Swiss families in the timber business. Young Bertha became interested in admission to Sweet Briar College. After her admission there around

1912, the entire family—Bertha, parents and grandparents—moved to Amherst. Her grandfather operated a dairy farm on the south end of town.

Bertha's father Henry Pfister, who spoke five languages, worked for several government agencies and at one point was the doorman for the U.S. Senate. After retirement from government service, he used his well-appointed basement workshop, which featured a work bench from Switzerland, to provide individuals, businesses, and the school shop with precision sharpening of knives, scissors, axes, and saws.

Bertha married Ben Wailes and was among the first three women ever named to the University of Virginia Board of Visitors in the 1940s.

• • •

Charles Younis arrived in Montebello, Nelson County, from Lebanon in 1920. He was a Christian and had graduated from Beirut University before coming to America. He lived with his uncle who had immigrated around 1910. Charles became an apprentice cabinet maker and helped build the school at Montebello. He taught

The Char-Del restaurant and gas station at the circle, around 1940.
Amherst New Era-Progress photo

for one year at the school.

He then moved to Lovingston and had a dealership for Model T Fords. In 1925, he came to Amherst, where he also sold Fords. When the traffic circle was completed in 1937, he built the Char-Del, named for himself and his wife, Della, whom he had met in Montebello. The Char-Del was a restaurant right at the crossroads of major highways, and served as a stop on the east–west Greyhound Bus Line.

• • •

Amherst's Greek presence involved two interconnected families. Paul Grekos had immigrated to New Hampshire early in the 20th century; he was a veteran of World War I. He married Eva, who was born in New Hampshire to Greek parents. When their first child arrived, Paul suggested that his sister Emily come from Greece to help in their home. Emily met her future husband, George Tsoleas, while in New Hampshire.

Both families moved south. In 1936, Mrs. Tsoleas and their five young children traveled to Greece to see the family. They were caught there in World War II, not returning until the war's conclusion. By this time, Paul Grekos had come to Amherst to open the Seminole Restaurant, a

favorite gathering place for many years.

George Tsoleas came a year later to open Ye Olde Travelers Inn, where another Greek had operated a restaurant. In 1945, Emily Tsoleas and the five children were finally reunited on Garland Avenue with George. The festive atmosphere of their reunion is still remembered by friends and neighbors. After her husband's death, Emily continued to operate the restaurant, where she was fondly known as "Mrs. George."

• • •

Ricardo Garcia and his wife Regla were hairdressers in a shop on the top floor of "the coffee shop" building. Richard had served as a pharmacist's assistant in Cuba before emigrating. Regla was a member of the Perez beautician family of Lynchburg, and Richard had at some point been affiliated in Spanish language education at Sweet Briar College. They had moved to Central Virginia well before the Castro Revolution in Cuba. The Garcias delighted in introducing their customers to two aspects of their former lives: enjoying Cuban food specialties and playing dominoes.

All were remembered as being proud of their native heritages, but equally proud of the lives they had built for their families in America. Even rural counties and small towns such as Amherst still offer prospects of opportunity to the world beyond their borders. ∞

BOARDING HOUSES SPAWNED LONG-TERM RELATIONSHIPS

By Leah Settle Gibbs

"Boarding house reach"—a pejorative term implying one's lack of manners at the dinner table—no doubt was a habit rarely employed in most of the boarding houses in Amherst in the mid-20th century. Those who recall those days do so with fondness of the home-like atmosphere, fairly formal living by today's standards and a foundation for lifelong memories and friendships.

The boarding house was an American institution—until home ownership and automobile transportation became commonplace, it provided convenient lodging near places of employment or schooling. In Amherst after 1900, many of the older two-story houses had several bedrooms, and the operation of a boarding house provided a necessary service. It was also a good way to supplement the household income. Many lifelong friendships and a number of marriages were launched as a result of the times spent in boarding houses.

Various professionals lived in boarding houses, some on a short term basis, as in the case of itinerant sales representatives or con-

The Bowman house, on the corner of Main Street and Hanger Road, served as a tourist home for many years.
Amherst County Historical Museum photo

struction and highway supervisors, while others boarded for several years. "Tourist homes" more often provided short-term lodging, often on just a daily basis for about $2 a day. Several Amherst homes displayed "tourist home" signs to acquaint passersby with the availability of lodging.

During World War II, when an Army division from Texas was training in the Lowesville area, some of the men and their wives filled Amherst boarding houses to capacity. One of

The Hanger house, a popular boarding house from the 1920s to the early 1960s
Sally Hanger Moravitz photo

PRESERVING AMHERST LANDSCAPES ON CANVAS

"Sally Fan" Hanger was about eight years old, she remembers, staying at her grandmother's, "Mrs. Hanger's Boarding House," for a summer visit in 1941. Two people she met were Horace Day and Elizabeth Nottingham, artists who would go into the Amherst countryside and paint by day, and be critiqued before dinner each evening.

One vivid recollection has remained with her, "I was in the room when they showed the 'Amherst Clay' picture. If I remember it right, it was just a clay bank with some plants and flowers. They would come in before supper and show what they had done. I looked at it and it appeared to be the same as it was the day before! But what's a kid to know? Well, they hadn't worked that day; they'd gotten engaged and had seen about the business of getting married!"

The Canonical Register of Ascension Church reveals that Horace Talmage Day and Mary Elizabeth Nottingham were married by John S. Wellford, rector of the church, on July 31, 1941, with Trueheart Poston, a local architect, and his wife, Martha Lee Poston, serving as witnesses.

In the early 1940s, Elizabeth Nottingham, an artist and alumna of the Randolph-Macon Woman's College class of 1928, returned to Central Virginia. Another painter whom she had met at the Art Students League in New York in the late 1920s was Horace Day, who joined her that summer in Amherst, staying at the Wade Wood house whose boarders took their meals at Mrs. Hanger's. The landscapes around them became subjects in their oils, watercolors, and drawings.

Two paintings, done concurrently on easels back-to-back, according to their son, Tal Day, show Amherst scenes and have been widely acclaimed; both are now part of the collection of the Virginia Museum of Fine Arts in Richmond. Nottingham's painting is "Country Road, Amherst, Virginia" and Day's is "Amherst Clay."

Elizabeth Nottingham (1907-1956) had aspired from childhood in Culpeper to be an artist and the rural scenes of Virginia were her special interest. Her education focused on that goal, with postgraduate work taking her to New York, where she gained a fellowship for further study in Europe.

In 1934, Nottingham's work was part of the "Public Works of Art Project Exhibition" in the Corcoran Gallery in Washington. One painting, "Culpeper Street," was purchased by Eleanor Roosevelt for the White House collection.

Horace Day (1909-1984), born in China to missionary parents, was trained in the latter '20s at the Art Students League in New York. He was acclaimed for his works whose themes often reflected his experiences in the American South during the 1930s. Soon after its completion, "Amherst Clay" was exhibited at the Carnegie Institute and subsequently traveled throughout the country with an "Artists for Victory" exhibition during World War II.

the longest-operating boarding houses was the Hanger home. Another was the Wade Wood house, currently the location of the Amherst County Historical Museum; the Wailes, Gregory, Robertson, and Voorhees homes were also boarding houses.

Several boarding houses were on Main Street, with others on streets just off Main, all centrally located. Young single lawyers and teachers, as well as a number of professionals at American Cyanamid, were among those living at the Wood and Hanger homes.

With wartime rationing of petroleum products, transportation was sometimes provided to American Cyanamid in Piney River. Teachers at Amherst High School or those who worked in downtown Amherst could easily walk to work.

With limited transportation options, or simply as a way to live closer to school during the week and generally return home on weekends, students maintained continuity in their schooling by boarding in town. During periods of severe weather conditions, some students from outlying areas would board because of travel difficulties. Many roads were unpaved and the ravages of rain and snow left the roads virtually impassable.

Life at the Hanger boarding house remains a vivid memory for Mary B. Stinnett, who lived there from 1948 to 1951. She was a home economics teacher at Amherst High School, having secured the job immediately after graduating from Madison College.

Other boarders at that time, either at Mrs. Hanger's or the Woods,' were Sarah Daughtry, a supervisor with the Amherst school system;

Their son, Tal, elaborates: "In Summer 1941, when Elizabeth Nottingham was staying in Amherst, she was scheduled to become professor of art at Mary Baldwin College that fall. During the '30s, after completing a fellowship for study abroad granted by the Art Students League, she was engaged in the various federal arts programs of the New Deal in Virginia: first, the Public Works of Art Program, then the Federal Art Project. In 1938-39, she became assistant director of the Virginia Federal Arts Project and moved at that time from Lynchburg to Richmond."

Tal Day continues the story. "I don't believe that either Elizabeth Nottingham or Horace Day was ever a long-term resident of Amherst, but it is possible that they painted in Amherst from time to time, both individually and when Horace Day visited Elizabeth Nottingham during the years before they married. But the significance of their time in Amherst cannot be diminished. During the six weeks that Horace Day and Elizabeth Nottingham were painting these two oils in Amherst, they decided to marry."

The son remembers visiting in Amherst long after his parents' boarding house days. His parents had apparently developed several enduring friendships as a result of this time in their careers.

Soon thereafter, the Days moved to Staunton where they became art teachers at Mary Baldwin College. Elizabeth painted numerous watercolors of Virginia landscapes, and these works, as well as drawings and oils, have been shown in exhibits extensively along the East Coast. Her works have appeared in at least twenty exhibitions at the Virginia Museum of Fine Arts. Works have also been included in exhibits on several occasions at the Whitney Museum of American Art in New York and at the

The Augusta Art Club and
Gertrude Herbert Institute of Art
506 Telfair Street
Augusta, Georgia

June 18 '41

Dear Elizabeth —

You must think me a very uncertain quantity — and I guess I have been lately, but now at last I will be free for a few weeks any way!

Yesterday I was examined by the doctors for the draft and have been told that it is unlikely that I will be called before July 10th; which leaves me still with time to visit you if I haven't

American Cyanamid employees Ellen Lee (Wailes), George Roe, Jim Bondurant, T. L. "Bud" Wright, Custis Carter, a teacher and later Cyanamid employee, who became Mrs. Wright; and Virginia Roller (Burks) of the Virginia Home Extension Service.

Boarders paid for rooms and meals, with a monthly charge $47 ($50 if weekends were included). Most boarders had their own bedrooms, although sharing rooms was occasionally the practice, as needed. Some houses provided a sink in each bedroom.

Lizzie Chambers worked in the house with Mrs. Hanger, and they both were involved with meal preparation and serving, as well as other household responsibilities. Mrs. Hanger's kitchen was outfitted with both an electric and wood stove, but one former resident reports that most of the cooking was done on "the old wood stove."

Residents of the Woods' boarding house took their meals at the Hanger home. Mrs. Hanger is remembered as being a genteel lady who walked, basket in hand, to Wade Wood's store on Main Street to acquire her groceries for the day.

Jean Higginbotham remembers that her grandmother, Olden Higginbotham, who lived on Mt. Olive Road, did laundry for the Wood and Hanger boarding houses. She especially recalls admiring the pretty dresses that some of the women boarders had.

Residents assembled for cocktail hour, then the hand bell rang to announce dinner. The later evening was passed with bridge or other games,

Amherst Clay, 1941
Horace Day (American, 1909-1984)
Virginia Museum of Fine Arts, Richmond. Gift of H. Talmage Day.
Photo: Katherine Wetzel © Virginia Museum of Fine Arts

Corcoran Gallery in Washington. Others are in collections at Ford Motor Company and the General Services. Administration, as well as those of Virginia colleges, including Randolph College, University of Virginia, and Mary Baldwin.

Horace Day became a professor of art at Mary Baldwin College after his time in Amherst, with his tenure being interrupted by service in World War II as a soldier, draftsman, and cartographer for the U.S. Army's 86th Division.

He returned to Mary Baldwin where he remained on the faculty until 1967. His works have been exhibited extensively in the East and numerous works are held in the collections of American museums, galleries, business headquarters, and universities, including Yale, University of Virginia, and United States Military Academy; Ford Motor Company, Metropolitan Museum of Art in New York, Whitney Museum of Art in New York, Chrysler Museum in Norfolk, and Virginia Museum of Fine Arts. Day's works were also exhibited at two World's Fairs, in San Francisco and New York.

Sally Hanger Moravitz now cherishes not only her memories of two distinguished artists whom she met in her youth, but also a pair of portraits of herself as an eight-year-old, one done by each of the artists residing in boarding houses in Amherst in the summer of 1941.

— Leah Settle Gibbs

Country Road, Amherst, Virginia, 1941
Elizabeth Nottingham (American, 1907-1956)
Virginia Museum of Fine Arts, Richmond. Gift of H. Talmage Day.
Photo: Katherine Wetzel © Virginia Museum of Fine Arts

The Wailes house, which served as a boarding house in the 1930s and '40s.
Paul Wailes III photo

Rate card from Green
Hedge Tourist Home
on North Main
Street.
Ella Hudson Cash photo

$1.50 – RATES –
– PER-PERSON –
– 3-IN-ROOM –
$2.00 – PER-PERSON –
– 2-IN-ROOM –

reading, or preparations for the next work day. When Mrs. Hanger was engaged with her regular bridge foursome, if a substitute was needed, one of the boarders could be pressed into service.

Bridge was a popular pastime in Amherst at that time, as it continues to be among many today. Sometimes there was a little dancing, accompanied by the radio or "Victrola."

When dates would call, Mrs. Hanger would always answer the door and summon the girl. Marriages or other lifelong friendships often grew out of the boarding house experiences, with a number of the people remaining in the Amherst area for the rest of their lives.

The day of the ubiquitous boarding house passed with a more mobile society and the advent of apartment buildings and increased availability of dining options. But the "reach" of the influence of life in boarding houses now stretches far beyond mid-century, with decades of memories and generations of people whose lives are forever intertwined through relationships fostered in that venue. ∽

The Green Hedge Tourist Home was operated by Norman and Stella Hudson.
Ella Hudson Cash photo

Virginia Reserve Militia: Front row: From left, Norman Patteson, Milton Drummond, DeWitt Evans, Paul Alphin, Caskie Lawhorne, Farrar Saunders, Chester Mays. Second row: Charlie Thompson, Stafford Douty, Ben Wailes, Bruce Ross, Gordon Proffitt, Dayton Storey, Lynwood Turner. Third row: Bob Bethel, Cary Nicholas, Webb Babcock, Joe Whitten, Maurice Gannaway, Walter Carter, unidentified. Fourth row: Van Miller, O.B. Ross, Parker Eskridge, Camm Drummond, Charles Younis, John Shrader, Jim Wood, Julius Lipscomb.
Ron Ritchie photo

Wartime

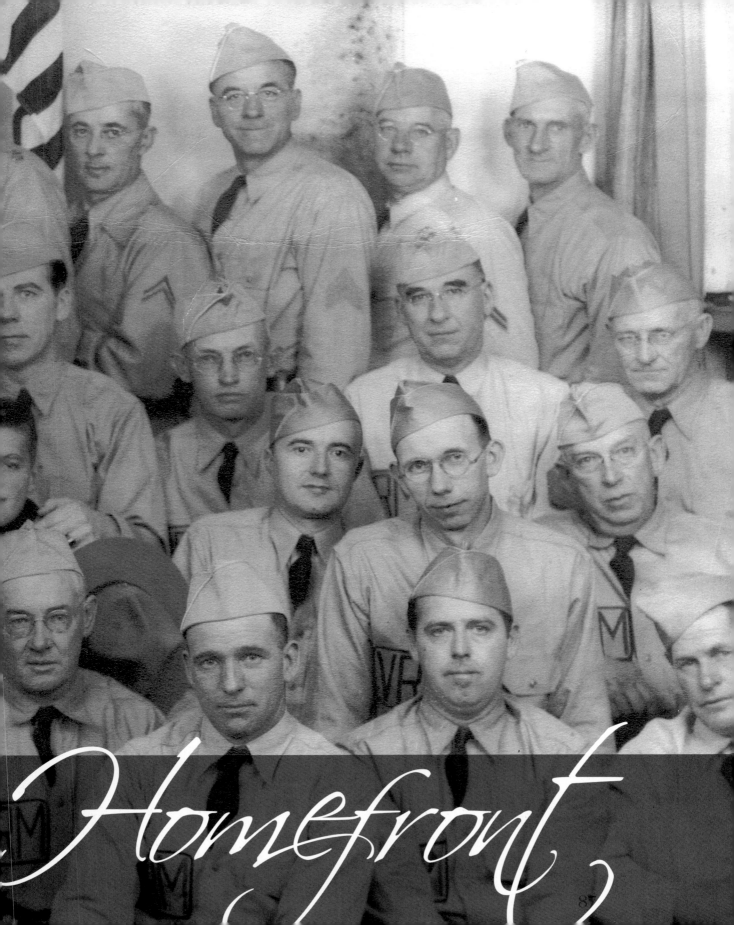

Homefront

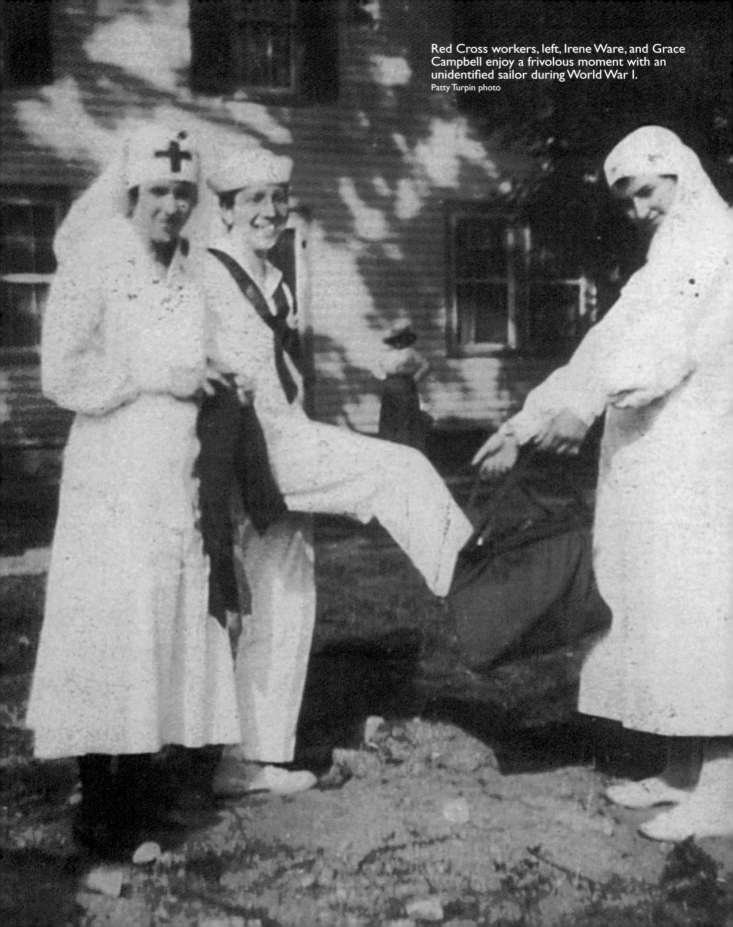

Red Cross workers, left, Irene Ware, and Grace Campbell enjoy a frivolous moment with an unidentified sailor during World War I.
Patty Turpin photo

FROM AN APPRECIATIVE SOLDIER IN 1918

By James D. Settle

Recently, America lost its last surviving veteran of what became known as World War I. At its end in 1918, after four horrific years of bloodshed and misery, it was usually dubbed "the World War" in the USA, "the Great War" in Britain and other countries—until 1939.

To this mostly-departed generation, 1918 also stands out for another, especially unpleasant memory: the influenza epidemic sweeping the Western world. In this country, it was known (for obscure reasons) as the Spanish flu—occasionally as the Swine flu. Generally thought to have been inadvertently spread by U.S. troops returning from the European battlefronts, it rapidly made its debilitating presence known virtually every-where in the country. By whatever name, it was frequently lethal.

Evelyn Ware Saunders, now 102, was ten years old at the time and became ill with the flu: "I can't remember ever being quite so sick, it was terrible. The schools were closed, and my sister, Irene, a teacher, was home to help. My brother, Julian, had been stricken by the flu and was unable to go into the Army. There was an entire family in Monroe that was ill. Two members of that family died. Julian would travel to Monroe by train to care for the family during the night in order to assist Papa (Dr. Ware) with their treatment."

The young Miss Ware's older sister Irene was also involved in the greater war effort, which touched Amherst, a cross-roads town, throughout the year and a half of American's participation. Army units—often "federalized" National Guard companies—passed through Amherst on their way to their bases, and meals and refreshments would be provided by the town's residents. One small resident, four-year-old Mary Dabney Meeks, remembered soldiers marching past her house singing the popular tune, "Goodbye, Liza Jane."

A young Reuben Higginbotham who served in France in World War I.
Jean Higginbotham photo

Irene Ware received a letter written by an appreciative soldier who had stopped in Amherst on his way north:

Hempstead, Long Island, New York
October 14, 1918

Dear Madam:

I take pleasure in writing you this evening and no doubt you are surprised to hear from me although I do not know who is getting this note.

If you remember the troop train that passed thru your city one day about noon by auto & trucks bound for up here, you people of the Red Cross and other places of business treated us very kind & I want to express my thanks for what kindness and courtesy we received while there those few minutes. I took a picture of a young lady there as you will see by the enclosed photo & as I was very neglectful on my part, I didn't get her name so as to send her a picture which she posed for me with the two plates of sandwiches. So I have taken this means of getting this picture to her, if you know who she is by her picture, I would be very glad & thank you for your trouble if you will find this young lady and ask her to accept this for her trouble. And I also thank you for your trouble. Again I express my thanks for the way you people of Amherst treated us all. Please let me know if you remember this girl & if she gets the picture. If she is unknown keep the picture as a souvenir of our short visit.
I remain respectfully,

Pvt. Ray D. Roseburrough
680th Aero Squadron
Aviation Field #2
Hempstead L. I., N. Y. ∽

D-DAY CLAIMS YOUNG DOCTOR

Captain Robert Ware
Patty Turpin photo

D-Day. The Sixth of June. The Normandy Invasion. The Great Invasion. "The Mighty Endeavor." "The Longest Day."

However they remember it—or have heard it—most Americans know the importance of June 6, 1944, the day Allied armies landed on the shores of Northern France to begin the liberation of Western Europe from Nazi Germany. What was the impact of this world-shaking event on the small rural town of Amherst, Virginia?

Among the thousands who fought, suffered, and died on those beaches were a number of Amherst County men, and one who fell, giving what Lincoln had called "the last full measure," was the doctor son of country practitioner and resident of the town of Amherst. Capt. Robert Ware, U.S. Army Medical Corps, was 28 years old when he was killed in the first hour of the day's savage fighting.

One of the ten children of Dr. Reuben Ware, a long-time physician, and 1933 graduate of Amherst High School, young Ware had graduated from VPI in 1937 and received his medical education at the Medical College of Virginia. In 1940, while on the staff at Lynchburg General Hospital, he joined the Virginia National Guard. Four years later, his unit went to war, and Ware was an officer-surgeon in the 1st Battalion.

Ware's commanding officer had offered him the option of not landing until the beachhead was secure. The young surgeon, though, had trained with the landing troops, and guessed that casualties would be heaviest in the first wave ashore. He would go in at H-Hour.

Bob Sales of Madison Heights, a radio operator on D-Day, recalls Capt. Ware's first, and last, moments on Omaha Beach: "Dr. Ware was one of the first off his craft and I could see a machine gun firing from the beach. It cut him down. He dropped right there." As Bob Sales, who was wounded, tells of his experiences, he remembers Ware's comment in choosing to be in the first wave, "That is where they will need me the most."

Capt. Ware left a young widow and two-year-old son. The valor and sacrifice that liberated a continent made a hero of a son of Amherst.

—*Adapted from an article by Paul M. Saunders, with permission by James D. Settle*

A TOWN THAT WAS READY DURING WORLD WAR II

By Leah Settle Gibbs

As the poignant story of Robert Ware indicates, the war for America's survival in the 1940s was an event that hit home everywhere. A town such as Amherst was not in the arena of combat, but many of its young men and women were, and virtually no one could remain untouched by it.

Many of the effects of the Great Depression disappeared with the country's total mobilization, but the need for frugality remained. Those too young for involvement in the war, or even knowledge of the issues, took part in its economies: drives for the collection of scrap metal, the cutting and folding of Red Cross bandages for the front, the knitting of Army green sweaters and vests for soldiers (these latter activities largely a women's effort, in such locales as John Shrader's store), and war bond rallies at the courthouse with speeches and music.

The people of Amherst experienced America's plunge into war from the outset. On Dec. 7, 1941, several U.S. Army convoys, including the 29th Division of later note on D-Day, were going north on Route 29, which,

at the time, was Main Street, Amherst. The resident highway engineer, Donald Selvage Sr., was meeting with the colonel in charge of the convoys, discussing road conditions and routes. The convoys generally passed rather slowly and methodically, continuing throughout the day, through towns along their route.

While Selvage and the colonel were talking, a young dispatcher was frantically trying to get the colonel's attention. He finally was able to deliver the message he had received via shortwave radio, that Pearl Harbor had been attacked.

The colonel quickly requisitioned a hand-lettered sign, "Japan attacks Pearl Harbor—Full Speed Ahead," to be placed at the traffic circle. The convoy at that point assumed open road speed, heading north to Indiantown Gap, Pa.

Within a mile of passing the traffic circle, the convoy was further informed of the magnitude of the events of the day. Several local boys—Ben Smith, Vic Hanger, Maurice and Tom Gannaway, Bill Olinger—were playing football in the Gannaways' yard. They came up with a light-colored wet substance, similar to plaster or

"Cricket" Webster is shown, right, with the rest of his crew, all of whom were casualties in a mid-air collision in Texas during a training mission.
Anne Day Garrison photo

cement or perhaps lime, and formed the letters in the road to say, "Japs bomb Pearl Harbor."

A woman who, as an early teenager, lived along Main Street recalled the passage of numerous convoys during the war. It was a fairly common practice for young girls to toss out wads of paper containing their names and addresses, hoping to develop a "pen pal" relationship with a soldier. Sometimes passing soldiers did the same for bystanders.

Marge Selvage Stone recalls having written to a Pennsylvania soldier throughout the war as he served in the Army in the Pacific Theatre. He returned from the war and went on with his life; she graduated from high school and college, married and moved elsewhere. These two people who had maintained this wartime correspondence never met—a story probably duplicated hundreds of times throughout the country. Jane Page Rothwell recalls having a similar experience with a soldier pen pal.

Paul Wailes III, in his early teens at the time, sums up, "The war changed everything about how we lived." Rationing or shortages

of everything, from automotive products and building supplies to food items, shoes and other "essentials" (including whiskey), became fairly universal. Amherst's ration office, located in the town office on Second Street, helped families keep tabs on the books of stamps used for legal purchase. Change was occasionally provided in "scrip" rather than coins, exchangeable for approved items.

Shortages of various commodities fueled everybody's efforts at making the most of what was available. Grain for livestock came in cotton sacks, in a variety of colors, prints, and patterns suitable for making clothing. Peggy Gregory Lau, a young girl of the '40s, recalls, "My mother carefully saved each sack until she had enough material to sew a dress or other item. Family and friends traded sack fabrics to have enough of the same fabric to make clothing. There was a shortage of elastic for sewing, so most of my clothing from underclothes to dresses had drawstrings.

"I had never seen chocolate until an uncle was discharged from the Army and came home with a duffle bag of goodies for the extended family. We gathered at my grandmother's home to await his arrival and it was like having Santa Claus opening his sack. I had my first taste of Hershey's chocolate bars and it was love at first bite. I recall the women were more interested in the nylon stockings and other scarce treasures."

An exotic treasure brought home by men who had served in the Pacific was the ever-popular grass skirt. Jean Higginbotham recalls just such a delight.

One boon to the economy of Amherst was afforded by the filling of boarding houses when an Army division out of Texas was training in the Lowesville area—geographically similar to parts of Italy where fighting was projected to begin in earnest.

Always with an awareness of the threat of invasion, localities prepared with various drills for such an eventuality. Peggy Lau elaborates: "I recall blackouts when the Amherst fire siren gave an alarm and everyone quickly pulled drapes and cut out lights so no light might be seen by the enemy. There would be neighborhood wardens assigned to make sure everyone complied. Sometimes we would go inside a closet or pantry that had a light to finish dinner or just to sit and await the 'all clear' signal."

Of course, Amherst was a long way from the world's battlefronts, but everybody felt part of what President Roosevelt called "our mighty endeavor." Other examples of individual initiatives—small perhaps in themselves, large in their evidence of commitment to a common effort, would follow.

Even though World War II was not fought on American soil, other than on the Pacific island territories, the potential threat was always felt and residents of the town of Amherst did their collective part to be ready. The threat of a German attack was perceived as very real, especially on the East Coast.

On the local level, a unit of the Virginia Reserve Militia, often called "Minutemen," was assembled as directed by Gov. Colgate Darden. Many of the men in town who were not in active military service because of a variety of factors—age, occupation, physical limitations, or other situations—gathered each weekend to train and be ready for local defense.

One of the local captains was Camm Drummond, a veteran of the Army Air Corps in World War I. These men drilled regularly and provided their own weapons and ammunition. The unit was prepared but never called to active duty.

Although automotive traffic was limited by rationing and a general lack of ownership of cars, those vehicles that were in use were required to have blackout covers on the headlights, which partially covered the light and directed it onto the road rather than outward. Some covered their headlights with black tape, leaving only a slit of light. People were almost universally compliant with participation in blackouts and other behaviors that were required in support of the war effort.

Observers manned specific sites to continually identify and report aircraft sightings. Many young people of that era dreamed of being heroic in some way; they had silhouettes of various aircraft hanging from their bedroom ceilings, faithfully learning each shape in an effort to recognize an enemy plane if the necessity ever arose. These alterations in daily lives remain today as vivid reminders to those who lived through that era—especially for children who would hear adult conversations about war, bombings, raids, invasions, and the ever-present threat of casualties.

It was hard to remain unaware of the battle fronts—listening to evening radio news became a family dinnertime ritual, with famous voices such as Ed Murrow, Lowell Thomas, Gabriel Heatter ("There's good news tonight!") and Walter Winchell ("Good evening, Mr. and Mrs.

Joseph Landon Parr
Betty Phillips Lupton photo

AMHERST MEN IN TUSKEGEE UNIT

Tournament of Roses Parade, New Year's Day 2010

Two native sons of Amherst served in World War II's most famous African American combat outfit, the legendary "Tuskegee Airmen" of the U.S. Army Air Forces in Europe. These flyers, recruited to serve as bomber escorts for the aircraft attacking Nazi-held North Africa and Europe, were trained at Tuskegee, Ala., and were active throughout the last two years of combat in the European Theatre of Operations.

Mitchell and Robert Higginbotham, brothers born in Amherst, moved to the Pittsburgh area of Pennsylvania at an early age with their family and volunteered for service in the Tuskegee unit early in the war. At war's end, they relocated west (Nevada and California), and, on New Year's Day 2010, participated in the Tournament of Roses Parade, riding with fellow veterans aboard a float decorated in honor of the Tuskegee Airmen.

The combat success of the Tuskegee unit, along with other African American outfits in World War II, would lead to the full racial integration of the U.S. Army, by executive order of President Truman in 1947.

—James D. Settle

America, from border to border and coast to coast and all the ships at sea") bringing reports of Europe and the Pacific.

War correspondents such as the great Ernie

> **To those young men of the town of Amherst who did not return:**
>
> **Capt. Robert Barnes Ware**
>
> **Lt. Frederick "Cricket" Charles Webster**
>
> **S/Sgt. Joseph Landon Parr**
>
> **PFC Herman Wright**

Pyle brought graphic combat details to daily newspapers (his book, *Here is Your War*, was also available). Pyle made the war very real to his readers, as one of the signatures of his writing was to cite each soldier's hometown. Even those seeking diversion at the movies sat through newsreels of the fighting.

As the last push to victory began in the

winter of 1944–45, the needs of the war hit Amherst as never before. By the end of the war, manpower requirements necessitated an accelerated rate of induction of young men into military service, leaving the Amherst High School class of 1945 with only four boys. Amherst residents remember the gathering of families at the depot, as they bade farewell to the next group of military inductees, their sons, brothers, and neighbors.

One local airman, Spotswood Allen, was training and his family knew he would be leaving soon for Europe. At a time known to his family, he buzzed the town, particularly his street (Garland Avenue), in his military aircraft, with his father standing in the yard waving his hat at him. Allen was later shot down over Germany, captured, and assigned to a prisoner of war camp. The Russians ultimately liberated the detainees from his POW camp. He then traded some cigarettes for a bicycle, whereupon he rode to a U.S. Army installation and found safe harbor.

A related national tragedy made its presence

felt in Amherst, with the death of President Franklin Roosevelt on April 12, 1945, at his retreat in Warm Springs, Ga. His casket was placed on a Southern Railway steam train; engines had to be changed at various locations, including Monroe. On its route back to Washington, the Roosevelt funeral train passed through Amherst in the early morning hours of April 14, arriving in Washington around 10 a.m. Roosevelt himself had always had affection for travel by rail, and this final journey allowed those along the way to pay respects to him at this pivotal time in the nation's history. .

In preparation for the arrival of this historic train the following day, one laborer who was loading cars at the Amherst depot is reported to have asked, "What time is President George Washington's train coming through tomorrow?"

A month later, May 8, the war ended in Europe with the surrender of the German armed force. With Japan's capitulation on Aug. 16, people jubilantly filled Amherst's streets or packed their families into cars and took off to join the celebrations in Lynchburg.

The most pivotal war in history had ended. In an evocative moment, as remembered by his daughters, one Amherst resident, Judge Edward Meeks, stepped onto his front porch and looked briefly to heaven with a silent prayer of gratitude. His only son, a veteran of heavy infantry combat from Normandy to the Rhine, was coming home. ∽

BARNEY & BOOTIE WYCKOFF

J. B. Wyckoff, known universally as "Barney," was a commanding presence in Amherst from the 1950s to the 1980s. Tall, red-haired, gregarious, a popular attorney, and a sought-after luncheon companion with a booming laugh. Grandson of the local Evans family of the Riverville area, he had spent summers in Amherst, and, on completing Navy service in WWII and U.Va. law school shortly thereafter, he set up practice in the town about 1950. His grandfather, Otto Lewis Evans, had been commonwealth's attorney in Amherst County for two decades.

The war years had brought him a wife, also in the Navy as a WAVE officer, who would become an Amherst personage in her own right. Lucretia—also known as **Bootie**—was a dedicated artist and a popular part of the local artistic circle. She taught many art classes to both children and adults in Central Virginia. Her watercolors and pastel portraits that still grace Central Virginia homes reflect how she lived, with flare and grand style.

Their deaths were tragic and untimely, but bound together—they lost their lives in a 1986 automobile accident. The memories, though, of this talented, energetic couple are ineradicable, as Barney is pictured with his long stride, walking to the courthouse with his suit coat flapping in the breeze, and Bootie charming art patrons with details of her most recent creations.

Barney Wyckoff

Cattle at the bottom of Scott's Hill, as shown in a watercolor by Bootie Wyckoff
Courtesy of Nancy McDearmon

95

Leisurely

Amherst Boy Scouts participating in a program in the Ascension Church parish house in 1954. From left; Jackie Ware, Richard Fink, Rod McPherson, Wally Masencup, Cliff Siegrist, Billy Jobe, Russell Addison, Bill Todd, Charles Higgins, Carl Miller, Dickie Sandidge, Donnie Woodson, Buddy Boon, Bobby Wimer, John Moore Wright, Jimmy McDearmon.
Bob Wimer photo

Pursuits

Amherst School talent show winners, around 1956. Seated, from left: John Rudacille, Bobby Wimer, Anne Sandidge, David Garland, Mike Morris, Jackie Banks. Standing, from left: Mary Todd, Phyllis Hesson, Steve Rudacille, Leonora Wikswo, Norma Jean Patteson, Billy Jobe, Peggy Gregory, Virginia Davis, Barbara Bowling, George Sullender, Shelby Allen.

A group of friends gather for an outing. Front, from left: unidentified, Jessie Thompson, and Tinsey Davis. Back, from left: unidentified, unidentified, Reuben Patteson, John Meredith Wright, and Troy Thompson.

Jean Higginbotham photo

FINDING FUN
IN A SMALL TOWN

By Leah Settle Gibbs

Roller skating. Dances over Wood's store. Cotillion parties. Climbing the water tank. Bicycling. TV as a family activity. Croquet and badminton. Forts in the woods. Movies. Amherst County Day. Church lawn parties.

Each era of young people in the town of Amherst has featured unique ways for having fun, usually associated with gatherings of family, school friends, and neighbors. Prior to society's increased mobility, home was the focal point of social gatherings, whether a family's Sunday dinner or a group of teens dancing to records at somebody's house.

Social boundaries were largely defined by the distance one was willing to walk or ride a bicycle. Those who grew up in the middle decades of the 20th century recall their freedom in circulating among friends' houses, going to various wooded areas to play in the creek or to build hideouts and forts. Family rules dictated limits.

Roller-skating on streets and sidewalks on Sunday afternoons was a favorite. Skates fit onto shoes and were adjusted by a key, which tight-ened the grips that clamped around the soles.

Groups would skate together down Court Street, then swing the person on the end around as they made the turn at Main. "I was always the shortest one, so I was on the end and would go swinging way out into the street," reports Helen Massie, happy to have survived the feat.

Sunday was also the day the family awaited its weekly amusement via "the funny papers." Life's everyday situations were caricatured to elicit a laugh about human nature. Adults could identify with "Maggie and Jiggs" in "Bringing Up Father," while the youngsters saw themselves in "Archie."

The 20th century opened the world of enter-tainment with the advent of "moving pictures" on the "silver screen," then its successor into most households, television.

Attending a movie in Lynchburg was a big event—early theaters were the Harrison, Warner, Isis, Academy, and Paramount. Many remember riding the bus to Lynchburg on Saturdays to watch a double feature.

One of the first epics in most people's memo-ries is *Gone With the Wind*, opening in the late 1930s. Wartime movies were coupled with news-

Teenagers gather in the Hudson home for a dance in the early 1960s. Pictured are, from left, Anne Dudley, John Scott Carter, (seated) Mildred Hopkins, Jane Hudson, Mary Cobb, Billy Jobe, unidentified, John Rudacille.
Ella Hudson Cash photo

A group representing the Home Demonstration Club on an outing to the Surrender Grounds at Appomattox. Back middle is Juanita Brown.
Jean Higginbotham photo

reels, the sources of both war news and patriotic messages. John Wayne served as everybody's "tough guy" hero and Clark Gable was the romantic leading man.

In Amherst, movies were shown on weekends in the health building. These events introduced many Amherst children to Hollywood: Laurel and Hardy or cowboy movies with Gene Autry and Roy Rogers. "I was a great fan of Gene Autry, as was my father. Once Gene Autry came to Lynchburg with his horse, Champion, and my father took my brother and me. I was thrilled." Such was Norma Jean Patteson Mills' touch with childhood idols.

Peggy Gregory Lau still laughs about her cousin standing up in a theater, yelling out, "Don't eat it! It's poison!," as the wicked stepmother hands the apple to Snow White.

One striking recollection of the entertainment world of the '50s was a trip to Lynchburg to a live performance by Boris Karloff as Frankenstein's monster. Karloff's trip off the stage and down the aisle etched an indelible memory, according to Mills, a young girl at the time, "It took me a long time to recover from that experience."

Jackie Ware remembers his school class being allowed to watch the coronation of Queen Elizabeth II, when a classmate's parents brought their TV to school in 1953. Later schoolroom viewing included the occasional World Series game, if the class behaved before game time.

Later in the 1950s, TVs had moved into most living rooms. Children were entertained in the afternoon by Howdy Doody, then Mickey Mouse Club. Sky King was heroic, and Sgt. Bilko amusing. Lessons of life were taught through "Leave it to Beaver" and "Father Knows Best."

Popular music was promoted by the ever-youthful Dick Clark on American Bandstand when Philadelphia teens rated a new tune, "It's got a good beat, easy to dance to. I give it an 85."

PISTOL PETE

One of the last "cowboys" in Amherst history was **Edward "Pistol Pete" Harrison** who actually received a ticket for racing through the town of Amherst on his favorite horse, Daisy. Harrison also entertained for years at the Amherst Fair where he would appear to shoot light bulbs thrown high into the air. He was an enthusiastic dancer of the polka when he accompanied his daughter Nancy to high school dances in the late 1950s.

Three school girls at Amherst Training School: unidentified, Pearl Wright, and Callie Reid.
Jean Higginbotham photo

Floyd Ward dance recital on the stage at the Amherst School around 1953. From left, Ryland Hunt, Marsha Hunt, Leah Settle, John Sam Payne, Pat Babcock, Jane Lewis.
Leah Settle Gibbs photo

Families gathered around the television after supper to laugh at the latest shenanigans of "The Honeymooners," with Jackie Gleason, or William Bendix in "Life of Riley." "Whadda revoltin' development dis is!" And the sage wisdom of Walter Brennan in "The Real McCoys."

More families had a car by the 1950s, and that fact, combined with the growing popularity of movies, launched "drive-in" theaters. The Amherst Drive-in provided a venue for a family activity—either a movie of universal appeal to include the children or a story for the adults, while the baby could sleep on the car seat. Parents would not have the expense of a baby sitter. Drive-ins sold refreshments and had a small playground for children before the show.

Ordinary citizens' introduction to political conventions began with television coverage in 1952—the nominations of Dwight Eisenhower and Adlai Stephenson. Besides the smoked-filled caucuses, backroom negotiating, multiple ballots, and party-rallying speeches, the public also experienced the peripheral scene of silly hats and waving banners, accompanied by "Happy Days are Here Again."

By the 1960s, television, automobiles, and other factors, meant that Amherst, like thousands of other American small towns, was no longer an island. But each resident of that "island" had his or her special memories of some individual delight.

Teens enjoyed gathering at friends' houses to play the latest records and dance. Young adults formed a cotillion club, which planned dances where dainty hors d'oeuvres would be served to partiers dressed in fine attire. Some remembered the little onion sandwiches. Amherst's disc jockey was Royal Ambler with his extensive record collection. Dances during the war years were held on Saturday nights above Wood's store.

A popular pastime in Amherst for much of the 20th century has been bridge playing. Women enjoyed the social outlet provided by numerous bi-monthly bridge clubs. Men also played regularly, either in "couples bridge," or in men's groups.

The fall and spring afforded opportunities for

The Leith house (current location of Fairmont Crossing) had the **first hard-surfaced tennis court** in Amherst.

101

Lunchtime at the counter at Glendale Pharmacy. Pictured on right is George Craig. Serving behind the counter is Judy Staton Dugan.
Amherst New Era-Progress photo

Soda fountains were located in Hatcher's Pharmacy and Glendale Pharmacy.

bridge luncheons. These events were held in private homes, at "Chinquapin," operated by Dorothy Dickey, "Town and Country Restaurant" in Madison Heights, or, later, at Winton Country Club.

Typical attire for these daytime events was a new suit or dress, with coordinating hat and gloves. Dishes of mints and nuts often complemented each table, and prizes of figurines and other knick-knacks were awarded for high and low scores. Such events generally made news in the following week's *Amherst New Era-Progress*.

One of the highlights of spring was the annual observance of Amherst County Day at Sweet Briar when the college opened its doors to the community. Some remember the Halloween-like atmosphere created in the science labs by the human skeleton hanging in a showcase.

School children eagerly anticipated the five-point parade, a celebration of an effort by the state departments of health and education to promote consistent practices in hygiene. Elementary students who met the criteria for good health in five categories were rewarded with participation

in the "five point parade." The five points were: weight, eyes, ears, teeth, and throat.

Fads in music, fashion, and interests have permeated every generation: penny loafers, saddle oxfords, hula hoops. Walt Disney elevated awareness of Davy Crockett's exploits, and Randy Wyckoff proudly wore his coonskin cap to Sunday School. Crinolines helped girls make a fashion statement with their full skirts—the more crinolines, the better.

Seasonal amusements included Halloween stunts, plus trick-or-treating. Peggy Gregory Lau remembers her home-made costumes, often as a hobo or gypsy, where tackiness was a desirable feature.

Vance Wilkins now admits to one of his favorite pranks: loading a paper bag with a fresh "cow pie," placing it on someone's sidewalk, setting it afire, then ringing the door bell and running off. Much merriment accompanied the perpetrators' viewing of this stunt from behind a nearby shrub, as the homeowner came out to stomp out the flames.

Big snowstorms provided opportunities for young people to gather along Scott's Hill, a long and winding route for sleigh riding. Bonfires provided the needed warmth and lighting for nighttime adventures on the slope. Stafford Douty provided a bobsled which sent many passengers speeding toward the bottom.

Even a church service's solemnity could be interrupted by a child's creative thinking, as reported again by Wilkins. Seated behind a bald-headed man, he would pull a thread from his socks and quietly tickle the man's dome just enough to get his attention. A quick swat at the offending "insect" would yield continued frustration, as the "pest" would return a few moments later, much to the delight of the kid in the pew behind him.

Another form of church-related entertainment came from a ladies' fashion trend of the '40s and

John Walter Reid Sr. and John Walter Reid Jr. get ready to mow the grass at their home on Mt. Olive Road.
Jean Higginbotham photo

The coronation of Patsy Phillips as "queen," a high achievement in the Girls' Auxiliary, a youth group at Amherst Baptist Church, mid-1940s.
Robbie Howell photo

'50s. Lau remembers, "Sometimes we sat behind a lady wearing a fox stole and I was fascinated and distracted by the little beady eyes and small face of the fox staring at us. Each of the animals seemed to be biting the other in the tail."

From the safety of a half-century and several thousand miles, Lau reported two more childhood adventures. The town water tower was strictly off limits, but featured a tempting metal ladder. A group of teenage girls was rewarded with the exhilaration of both a panoramic view and the challenge and feat itself. They succeeded in ascending and descending without incident and never attempted it again.

Likewise, the fire alarm button in the telephone office, conveniently located in the home of a friend's grandmother, proved too much to ignore. It was reported as an accidental pulling of the switch when the operator was out of the room. The alarm sounded, summoning firemen into action, much to the consternation of two little girls who were merely investigating the possibilities. A firm scolding seemed to have been the only punishment, with the lesson learned.

Amherst was no different from other Virginia towns that were coming of age in the 1950s. It did have a pool hall. And, as usual, some of the youngsters who frequented it probably would have been better off completing their homework assignments for the next day.

The pool hall was located in the second floor space above what is now Designs by Robin and Montague Miller & Co., the real estate firm on

HONEY THE DOG

Jack and Judy Faris' dog "Honey," a yellow Lab, followed cars along Sunset Drive, sometimes venturing into town, to the high school, and even to Sweet Briar, where students welcomed her into the dorms.

When they moved west of town, Honey continued her wandering ways. She would follow Phillip Moore, a frequent pedestrian, as he went into town. The Farises soon learned that Honey's motivation for her travels was the supply of pork chops often found behind Drummond's store.

Honey's new venue left her in a quandary for returning home, so she learned to sit in the Amherst traffic circle to await Jack's daily return from work. Depending upon his mood at the moment, Jack would either give Honey a ride or make her follow the car all the way home.

Later in life, Honey's roaming diminished. She would travel only a couple of miles, to the end of Christian Springs Road, to sit in the Drummonds' yard to await her master's return, with the subsequent ride home.

103

South Main Street. Big windows that overlooked Main Street were usually open so the players could watch the traffic on Route 29 coming through town.

As Johnny Wimer recollected, a game of pool could be played by putting your 15 cents on the rail of one of the eight pool tables. A tap of the cue on the old wooden floor would bring a fellow who went by the name of "String" over to rack the balls. String, as his name implies, was tall and lanky. It was unusual for him to smile at his customers and his usual response to the tap of the cue was, "I'll get there as soon as I can."

When the phone would ring, the usual response from those at the tables was, "I'm not here."

Wimer recalled that the money game was 9-ball played by the best shooters who would gather around the first table to the right by the window in the front.

And what would those who had had enough pool do to while away the rest of the afternoon or evening? Why they would go up to the Gulf station at the traffic circle and hang out there for awhile. That was the good life.

Funny, scary, accidental, legal or illegal—all memories were recalled with equal certainty and verve. Those who grew up in the town of Amherst found myriad sources of amusement. It can be a quick flash or an extended reverie, but a lot of Amherst residents can attest that memory grows more vivid with age. It was oft said, "Glad we lived to tell about that one . . ." ∞

EDDIE THE CROW

The Gordon Dearborns had a pet crow named Eddie. He was named after Dr. Sandidge who had given the crow to the family. Eddie would follow the children to school. In the days before air conditioning, the school windows would be open and Eddie would fly into classrooms and steal pencils. He also accompanied Lloyd Dearborn into town for Sunday afternoon rollerskating; one time, he took Helen Massie's skate key and never returned it.

AT MID-CENTURY,
A CHILD'S GLIMPSE OF AMHERST

By Patty Walton Turpin

Life was simpler in the late 1940s and early 1950s. Almost everything in the town of Amherst was within walking distance. The world was within a bike ride or a hop, skip, and a jump away. Parents knew their children felt safe and confident, walking to and from school. Some children even came home at lunchtime or stopped for a snack on the way home in the afternoon.

Now as my contemporaries and I walk through town in our minds, more than five decades later, names and faces quickly come into view. Childhood memories do not necessarily focus on the person in charge of an office or business, but sometimes on the first person to greet the unsuspecting six-year-old. The passage of time does not diminish recollections of the sights, sounds, and smells of the buildings.

If medical assistance was needed, Dr. Ray Arnold and Dr. Lyddane Miller were available. The human skull in a cabinet in Dr. Miller's office always attracted attention. Both doctors had nurse assistants, Dorothy Mosby in Dr. Miller's office and Virginia White in Dr. Arnold's. They were consummate professionals with their freshly starched uniforms and gentle manner.

They could soothe a child's anxiety or deliver advice to a worried parent. Dorothy watched the three Miller children grow up. Nancy Miller Smith recalls that Dorothy once kept a watchful eye for the arrival of a mail-order pet skunk, Gardenia X. Stinko. Mrs. Mosby continued her medical career in Dr. Gordon Leonard's office and saw the next generations of Amherst children coming for their pre-school exams and shots.

Virginia White's daughter, Cynthia, cited instances in her childhood when Dr. Arnold's patients would come to their home at all hours for such services as insulin shots. Mrs. White later became a licensed professional nurse at Ryan's Nursing Home.

The Health Department was an important institution for routine immunizations. Children sometimes walked from school to the health building for polio shots in the 1950s. The mobile x-ray unit gave the annual dose of radiation. Tuberculosis was in the back of parents' minds, therefore it was stressed that an x-ray was needed. Nurse Edna Burton was there to

A group of teens gathers to celebrate the 16th birthday of Mary Frances Davis in 1956.
Jean Higginbotham photo

Ella Hudson's birthday party, around 1950. From left, Patty Ogden, Paula Catlett, Frances Simpson, unidentified, Anne Dudley, (almost obscured) Ella Hudson, Barbara Wilsher, Jane Hudson, (foreground) Jamie Wright, Barbara Jones, Nancy Burks, Betty Hunt.
Ella Hudson Cash photo

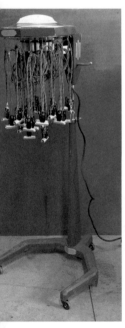

People who went to the Garcias' beauty shop in the 1940s and '50s remember a hair curling machine similar to this one.

assist putting on the special x-ray outfit. Nurse Burton, with a warm smile and her neatly pressed uniform, gave youngsters a secure feeling about shots and x-rays.

Frequently seen around Main Street was a man with the melodious name of Piccolo Jackson, always smiling—a man who could recite unique and interesting poetry and was never shy about sharing his most recent work with you. Families relied on Piccolo for performing odd jobs around their homes. He was more than willing to accept unwanted items and sell them along the way. He typified the complete definition of "handyman."

Another memorable person around town was Willie Rose. Ben Smith swears the man could "whistle in four-part harmony."

A treat was a visit to Bethel's watch and clock repair shop. Watches and all sorts of clocks lined the shelves and glass counters in his shop, along with sparkling jewelry. These items provided great fascination, as cuckoos and chimes chirped and clanged constantly. Robert Bethel studied clock repair in library books on his own time for seven years while he worked for the Virginia Department of Highways.

Bethel was well-known, often receiving old clocks from all over the country. He made many of the parts himself, especially the wheels and bushings. Bethel smoked a cherry tobacco pipe as he peered through little magnification

glasses, which rested on the end of his nose. His curiosity and ingenuity were legendary as he loved the challenge of repairing any watch, clock, radio, or piece of jewelry brought in.

Town residents kept Chester's shoe repair shop humming. Chester Rucker learned his trade from Clarence Camden and began his own business in his home on Main Street in 1961. It was great fun to watch Chester work on shoes, although it could be noisy in his shop accented by the sweet aroma of leather and oils. There were always stacks of shoes waiting for the owners to pick them up.

Another stop in town would be Joe Whitten's barber shop. Little girls got their Buster Brown trims there so the barber shop was not just for boys and men. The trim was complete once Whitten swept the sweet-smelling soft brush across the back of the neck. Little boys would marvel at the conversation and easy banter that went on among adult customers.

Mothers would enter the coffee shop building to ascend two flights of stairs to the Garcias' "beauty parlor." The scent of permanent wave solution permeated the entire stairwell. A memorable sight in the shop was like something from *I Love Lucy*. It was a permanent wave machine, almost indescribable—sort of a flat-topped tree—a disc maybe two feet in diameter atop a pole in a base, and from this disc hung a dozen or more electric cords, each

106

tipped with a hair clip. Each of these clips was placed on a curl, and the lady would ultimately be hooked to all of them for a period with heat flowing through the contraption.

The new Drummond's store, built in 1953, was a place to see one of the Day family's pony-sized dogs lounging on the sidewalk. The dog would be waiting for a snack or for recess time at Amherst Elementary and Amherst Training School, where he enjoyed lots of attention.

A plumbing or electrical problem at home meant a call to Raymond Gregory, who, along with his assistant, Billy Turner, would respond to evaluate and repair the trouble. According to Gregory's daughter Peggy, Billy was born with restricted arm and hand development. A hip problem caused a limp. Gregory always said that Billy could do the work better than any person who had full use of limbs; he compensated for limitations with tremendous versatility and skill.

A trip to the dentist was always eased by the thought of a post-exam treat. Dr. David Amowitz's office was above Shrader's store and he rewarded young patients with a coupon redeemable for a popsicle at the store. The office also provided entertainment in the form of a good selection of comics. Peggy Gregory Lau admits to dropping by the office on the way home from school just to check on the latest adventures of *Captain Marvel, Archie*, or *Mutt and Jeff*.

Another young patient recalls that Dr. Amowitz would always remark about the squeaking sound as he packed in a filling, "That sounds like a new pair of Easter shoes, doesn't it?"

The most frequently utilized social and meeting hall was the parish house of Ascension Church. Halloween parties, Floyd Ward dancing lessons in tap, ballet, and ballroom, Boy Scout meetings, and other commu-

nity events occurred at the parish house. One obscure memory of ballroom dances, generally involving sixth or seventh graders, was the fact that the boys had to wear short white gloves. These were regularly borrowed from Wright's Funeral Home, because their pallbearers wore them as they served in that capacity. Girls wore elbow-length gloves for the ballroom finale.

Vance Wilkins recalled playing "table hockey" at Boy Scout meetings at the Parish House in the 1940s. The game involved using two overturned tables as goals, one at each end of the large meeting room; the legs provided the framework of the goal. Boys scrambled to strike a tennis ball with an open hand to knock it into the goal—a combination of hockey and team handball, with a lot of youthful male roughness thrown in.

A small kindergarten was also held in the parish house for several years in the 1950s, before kindergarten became part of the public school system.

At the post office, Gates Ware was an institution. He walked to work from his home on Hanger Road. The post office at that time was located on Main Street next to the bank—currently Elkwood hair salon. As postmaster, he hired many a youngster with a bicycle to deliver special delivery letters.

Memories of the people with whom a child came in contact—townspeople on their daily rounds, buying groceries, going to the courthouse, meeting for lunch, or picking up mail—are clearly embedded for a lifetime. Sixty years later in a fast-paced world, one cherishes indelible thoughts of a time when almost everybody who passed on the street knew each other and life seemed safe and secure. ∞

Joe Whitten puts the finishing touches on a haircut for Billy Edgemon. The sign at the back of the shop lists prices: Hair Cut Prices, Weekdays 50¢, Saturdays 65¢, Shave 35¢, Saturdays 40¢.
Susan O'Neil photo

ATHLETICS, ALWAYS WITH A SMILE ON MAIN STREET

For those who knew him, the name Gates Ware brings to mind one subject: sports. No matter what the activity, he was an avid sportsman. And nowhere would you find a friendlier person with whom to engage in a sport—whether as a participant, coach or spectator.

For me, Gates Ware will always be remembered as the Amherst postmaster. Because his son, Jack, and I were classmates through elementary and high school, it was also my privilege to be closely acquainted with "Mr. Ware," the title of respect we always accorded him. To his contemporaries, he was simply "Gates."

Arthur Gates Ware Jr. loved athletic competition. He and a group of friends were among the first in Amherst to play golf on a regular basis, traveling as far as necessary to courses throughout Central Virginia. In the mid-1950s there were few public courses near here. He was a charter member of Winton Country Club and spent many an afternoon on the golf course there after it was completed more than a decade later.

A group of men engaged in a croquet match on the grounds located behind the court-house. Weekend croquet play moved to a site near Main Street in the early 1940s.
Top: Arthur Gates Ware
Amherst County Historical Museum photos

On weekends, he and his friends would stay in town and play croquet or pitch horseshoes.

When Jack and I played youth league baseball and basketball, we could always count on his dad to be at the games and at as many practices as possible. Mr. Ware would also work with us after hours, hitting grounders and pop flies in hopes that we would improve our play in the field.

His encouragement was such that I was sure that if I stayed with the game, the major leagues would be within my reach despite my considerable deficiencies.

While winning was important to Mr. Ware, I recall that how we played the game was more important. Good defensive plays and a solid performance at the plate were far more important than the final score. And arguing with the umpire, a role he filled from time to time, was out of the question.

He gave us a deep appreciation for baseball. But no matter what the game, he taught us to play by the rules and respect those in authority.

From the main window of the old post office across the street from Hill Hardware on Main Street—a building with columns that to most youngsters seemed as high as the sky—Mr. Ware greeted his customers with a smile and a twinkle in his eye. That twinkle grew brighter around children, all of whom he loved and loved to tease.

If you had just gotten a haircut, and in those days when you got a haircut it was obvious, he would ask you when you were going to get a haircut. If you were breaking in a new pair of shoes, he would ask you when you were going to shine them.

At times, he would grab your upper arm between his thumb and index finger and squeeze until he got a response. And then laugh like crazy.

In my adult years, he simply greeted me with that huge smile of his and often would ask, "Do you feel as good as you look?" Or a variation of sorts.

When I returned to Amherst nearly 40 years ago, I remember going down to the post office and asking Mr. Ware for a post box. "How about the 'Wreck of the Old '97?" he asked. I still have Box 97.

By then the post office had moved into a new building across the street and a block of so north of the old one.

Gates Ware, who died in December 1990, was one of a kind. His cheery smile and words of encouragement enriched the lives of all who were privileged to know him or to be associated with him. He was one of Amherst's many true gentlemen.

—Robert Wimer

WEEKEND CROQUET MATCHES

By Leah Settle Gibbs

"It was the most fun for the least amount of money anybody could imagine."
—*Harold Higgins, age 92*

Weekly croquet games in an empty lot just off Main Street between the Hanger and Wood houses provided a decades-long pleasure for many Amherst men who gathered there with hand-made croquet mallets, balls, wickets, and posts. It wasn't, though, the aimless knocking of a wooden ball through wickets—the games were usually played on Saturday and Sunday afternoons, and the competition could be serious and intense at times.

The croquet competition began years earlier on a course laid out by Lucian H. Shrader on his property near the court house. The games moved from there to the Main Street site in the early 1940s.

A men's croquet league also played at Miller Park in Lynchburg on a dirt surface surrounded by "bang boards" for boundaries. The Amherst men played on a grass surface, the dimensions of which were recently approximated at 150 feet by 85 feet. The boundary was delineated by a heavy-gauge wire buried a couple of inches beneath the

surface around the perimeter. It could be found by a player slipping a pocket knife blade into the ground to find the boundary if a ball went out-of-bounds.

The mallets were handmade, many by regular players Harold Higgins and Stewart Floyd, both talented woodworkers in Amherst. Mallets were generally made of red oak, with a few being walnut. One end of the striking surface of the mallet was wood with a leather cap. The other end was covered by a hard rubber pad about an inch thick, made from stoppers from containers used at the American Cyanamid plant in Piney River. These rubber additions were glued on and held in place by a metal band around the mallet head. A similar band encircled the wooden end, as well, to secure the leather cover and to help prevent splitting of the wood.

Players used the rubber or hard end to strike the ball for very specific reasons. When a player's ball struck another ball, the player could use his bonus strokes to move both his ball and the other, which were placed next to each other, with the striker's ball being the one he would hit:

One of Higgins' handmade mallets.
Leah Settle Gibbs photo

Harold Higgins, who often played in the weekend croquet matches of the 1940s, '50s, and '60s.

One of Higgins' handmade mallets.
Leah Settle Gibbs photos

the wooden end of the mallet would "roquet" the balls in such a way that the lead ball would go considerably farther than the struck ball; the rubber end of the mallet would cause an effect wherein both balls would travel similar distances. Players could position the striking ball in such a way that the balls could travel a similar route, or go in different directions, depending upon strategy.

Another option upon hitting another's ball was to secure the player's own ball against the other, holding it in place with his hand while striking both to send the other's ball in a particular direction, while keeping his own ball in place for the next bonus stroke. "Backyard" play generally has one securing his ball with his foot rather than his hand.

Most games involved four players—either "every man for himself," or playing as partners, two against two. Games could involve intricate strategy and last for as long as two hours.

The wickets were made of heavy-gauge wire and were situated in a more spread configuration than most backyard set-ups and included a "cage" for the middle wicket. This cage consisted of two crossing wickets and the players had to make the wicket in a diagonal direction.

Players, by rule, had to use a one-handed stroke, in one of two styles: either sideways to the projected path of the ball (similar to a typical putt in golf), or squarely facing the direction of the ball, stroking the mallet beside the right leg (if right-handed). Most players used the sideways approach, but always one-handed (never the between-the-legs style of most backyard players).

These croquet games were played almost year 'round. Other than materials for initial equipment, the only other expense incurred by the players was in maintaining the field. They acquired a lawnmower and employed a local youth to mow the field regularly. The weekend competitions continued into winter weather, with one recollection of a player who worked in the construc-

tion business bringing in several large kerosene heaters, each about eight feet tall and placing them strategically around the court. The players would take their turns, then return to the warmth of the nearest space heater.

Tommy Littrell, who lived nearby, found the croquet grounds and games to be a good source of revenue: he occasionally painted the wickets for the players, and in the summertime, he sold lemonade for their refreshment.

In the earliest days, the players would play in their regular business attire. Unfortunately, no photograph is known to exist of the day that James E. Bowman, in his dark trousers, starched white shirt, dark tie, and bowler hat, played in the rain, with a croquet mallet in one hand and large black umbrella in the other.

Mr. Higgins' recollections were that the best player in his era was Harry Faulconer Sr., whom he described as precise in his play but gentlemanly in every way; second best was Arthur Gates Ware, Amherst postmaster, who lived near the croquet field. Other players included Harry Loftus, Buddy Schirmacher, Larry Littrell, Willie Bowles, John Hopkins Sr., Will Mays, Dr. Lyddane Miller, Dr. Edward Sandidge, Dick Faulconer, Bill Ellinger Sr., Charlie Smith, Charles Phillips, and Jake Stone. Games often were discussed at length following the conclusion, with considerable analysis of each stroke and strategic maneuver.

The weekly Amherst croquet matches gradually drew to a close in the 1960s, after several decades of play. The ownership of the playing field changed hands and natural attrition prevailed, as the group failed to attract new players at a time when greater mobility allowed people to travel farther from town for entertainment. Youth sports also grew in popularity, necessitating parental leadership, and interests changed with the growing popularity of golf and tennis in the area.

But, for many a summer afternoon, Amherst had been enlivened by a simple game, played with style. ∞

A FESTIVAL CELEBRATING PULPWOOD

By Robert C. Wimer

In what was billed as one of the most colorful events in the history of the town of Amherst, the week-long Virginia Pulpwood Festival made its debut on April 21, 1955. A highlight of the festival was a mile-long parade through downtown Amherst, featuring floats, old cars, horse-drawn buggies, four marching bands and trucks loaded with pulpwood. It attracted more than 2,500 people on a Saturday morning.

A parade with pulpwood trucks? A pulpwood festival?

You must understand that at the time Amherst County was the leading pulpwood producer in Virginia. Cutting pulpwood—mostly pine—was a labor-intensive industry that involved felling the trees, trimming off the limbs, sawing the remains of the tree into five-foot-long logs and loading them onto a truck.

It was hot, dirty work with the only mechanical assistance coming in the form of a power chain saw. The financial reward was obviously decent at the time, although it pales by comparison to today's wages. Pulpwood dealers paid the munificent sum of $16 for a cord of wood. And that included loading the logs onto specially built train cars at sidings in Amherst, Sweet Briar and Monroe.

The logs were then hauled by train to a variety of paper mills around Virginia where they were processed into wood pulp and eventually paper. Among the mills, which sponsored a float in the parade, were Chesapeake Corp. in West Point, Mead Corp. in Lynchburg, West Virginia Pulp and Paper in Covington, and National Container Corp. in Big Island.

The festival, which spanned a week in late April for several years, was sponsored by the Amherst Junior Chamber of Commerce. J. Bernard McDearmon, president of the Jaycees, acknowledged the financial support of paper mills around the state for the festival in a 1956 program and added, "The Jaycees, in planning the original pulpwood festival, stressed the fact that the most important function of the week-long celebration would be to emphasize the importance of pulpwood to the economy of Amherst County and similar counties throughout the state."

By 1956, the parade had expanded to six marching bands and drew what the *Amherst*

111

As I write this story, I am not sure that my editor will accept it. My assignments have related to facets of Amherst history, and here I am, writing a narrative on a dog. Not an ordinary dog, mind you, but an extraordinary purebred collie named Laddie. I was fourteen and a paper boy whose morning route took me down Garland Avenue.

There were no vicious, growling, threatening dogs on my route, but this handsome and sweet collie must have sensed that I had read Albert Payson Terhune's book on collies. He would accompany me on my route and eventually adopted my family. His owner, an elderly lady, said he had just shown up at her house a year earlier but that they had never really bonded. So the boy and the dog became real pals.

Laddie even graced Mrs. Myers' annual Latin Banquet after Sally McClenny and I spent the afternoon bathing him. He was resplendent in his luxuriant collie coat, lacking only a toga!

Every night Laddie would sleep outside my bedroom window at the Baptist parsonage. It was comforting to hear his rare bark, sounded only if something or someone had entered the yard. On Sunday morning, Laddie would often greet the faithful as they arrived or left the church. He was well known all over town.

So on that August 1961 night when he was struck by a car just south of town, someone knew to call me. I called the local vet and he met me there. The diagnosis was grim: a broken back and serious internal injuries. I had two choices: the vet could euthanize him or I could take him home to die there, certainly by morning. I chose the latter.

We placed Laddie in a low cut-out box and the vet perhaps gave him a pain killer. I really can't recall. After many painful minutes, saying my last good byes to my faithful chum, I went to my bed in the adjoining room and fell into a merciful sleep.

And then I was awakened to the sounds of something dragging itself across the floor to my low bed. When I turned on the light, Laddie's sweet, big brown eyes and muzzle were inches from my face. I cried out and Laddie, after that last full measure of devotion, sank to the floor dead.

I was 18, just a few weeks before I was to leave for college; I walked outside into the night and wept like a small child. I am now 67 and I have owned many collies since then. But I have never found another Laddie.

—Thurman Davis

Lemon Johns prepares to lead Marion McDearmon and his pony, Toby, in the Pulpwood Festival Parade. Festival officials are riding in Stafford Douty's 1923 Dodge Touring Car. At right is Bob Sales.
McDearmon family photo

THE AMHERST
JUNIOR CHAMBER OF COMMERCE
Proudly Presents
THE VIRGINIA
PULPWOOD FESTIVAL

New-Era Progress reported to be the largest crowd ever to turn out for an event in town—8,000 people. "Both sides of Main Street were lined from the south end of town to the entrance of the road leading to the fairgrounds (off Hanger Road) where festivities continued until midnight to conclude the week-long festival." The parade, which included the festival queen who had been crowned the night before with much ceremony at Buck's Place on Route 29, had assembled at Tommie's Inn, now the Briar Patch, south of town.

While the parade was undoubtedly the most spectacular part of the festival, numerous events were staged during the week to sustain the festival and its theme. A carnival cranked up each night at the fairgrounds beginning at 7 p.m. A jousting tournament that attracted entrants from all over the state was held on the afternoon of the parade with the winning knight's lady being crowned at the Saturday night tournament ball at the fairgrounds exhibit hall.

A flower show, horse show and greased pig contest filled in other time slots during the festival days.

Cowboy Copas and his Oklahoma Cowboys appeared at the fairgrounds for two shows in 1956. The country music stars brought their act to Amherst from the Grand Ole Opry of Nashville.

Wood cutting and chopping contests provided another highlight of the annual festivals. The Thursday night event featured contestants competing against the clock to see who was the fastest in power sawing, buck sawing and axe chopping.

Power saws were limited to those of five horsepower or less and no dealers were allowed to enter contestants with new saws. All contestants must have owned their own saws or used one belonging to a person other than a dealer for whom they worked. The contests carried a 50-cent entry fee.

According to news reports, Carlton Pugh of Amherst won the first power saw contest by slashing through a 14-inch red oak in 22 seconds. In the buck saw and chopping contest, Duvall Sandidge of Clifford walked off with top honors. The youngster cut through a 14-inch oak with his buck saw in 39 seconds, faster than some contestants did with the power saw. He won the axe-chopping competition with a time of two minutes and 35 seconds, a feat that was described as the most spectacular of the day.

Children were even excused from school on Friday afternoon (with a note of approval from their parents) to attend special children's day features that included a Smokey Bear show. All carnival rides were offered to the children at half price.

An interesting sign of the times appeared on the side of the Virginia Forest Service's Smokey Bear float in the 1955 festival parade. "Crush Your Cigarette," it advised, and be a "champ like Smokey!" Cigarette smoking was obviously more acceptable in those days.

The Virginia Pulpwood Festival enjoyed a run of about four years. It was an entertaining event for children and adults in town and a pleasant diversion from the hard and not so glamorous work of the enterprise it celebrated—cutting, loading and shipping pulpwood. ∞

Lemon Johns leads Marion McDearmon on Toby through town in the Pulpwood Festival parade in 1956. *Amherst New Era-Progress photo*

Dr. and Mrs. R. B. Ware, center, at Amherst
County Fair tournament ball in 1915.
Patty Turpin photo

(bottom) A group of local residents aboard
a wagon, heading to the Amherst County
Fair in 1914.
Amherst County Historical Museum photo

Amherst County Fair
1924
Pass
To Tournament Ball.
L. H. SHRADER, Chairman.
Countersigned by

THE COUNTY FAIR:
A WELCOME ANNUAL DIVERSION

By Leah Settle Gibbs

For young and old alike, the County Fairs were among the most anticipated local events of the year. Segregated fairs were held during the first half of the 20th century, with whites attending the one at the Amherst Fairgrounds off the present Hanger Road, and blacks holding theirs at Gordon's Fairgrounds located in the area east of Amherst bearing a road by the same name, the current location of Amherst Middle School.

These annual events provided a social outlet featuring a variety of shows and activities for all ages and interests.

The Amherst Fair was started around 1910 as a stockholders organization, purchasing property and erecting basic structures. One of these buildings fell victim to an ice storm in 1934, when its roof collapsed. Paul Wailes III recalls a constable, Hamm Kerr, cutting a rather dignified and imposing figure in the '30s in his ten-gallon hat and five-point badge that seemed to fill half his chest.

The week-long celebration occurred in the fall, a time for the townspeople and those from nearby areas to take a deserved break from farm labors, to exhibit various homemade specialties in food and crafts, to exhibit prized farm animals, and generally to experience a relaxing social occasion with neighbors. Many of the activities could hold a child's interest for hours. The school children eagerly anticipated a scheduled half-day vacation for the event.

Among those with the clearest recollections of the fair were people who lived near the grounds. They could observe the fair start to finish. One who lived near the Amherst Fairgrounds would tell his children about being so fascinated "when the Gypsies would come to town." Whether the carnival people were truly Gypsies or whether the term was used more to imply a group of people who moved from place to place, living in temporary housing, selling their wares and providing exotic-looking prizes for feats of skill at the entertainment booths, is difficult to determine. Regardless, their arrival signaled a week of fun-filled promise.

One resident who lived on Hanger Road, Tommy Littrell, has provided a narrative of his recollections, and, in some cases, confessions.

"I have vivid memories of the fairgrounds

GLADYS TALIAFERRO

Many recall the little woman who drove the 1939 Plymouth Coupe for several decades. **Gladys Taliaferro** was the granddaughter of an Episcopal minister and daughter of a claims agent with the N&W Railroad, who were equally legendary.

Miss Taliaferro had been sent "up north" to college, then was employed in the Washington, D.C., area in the field of social work.

After she returned to Main Street, Amherst, in the 1940s to care for her aging mother, she opened a small kindergarten in the little building next to the Robertson house.

She was well-versed in the history of Amherst County, but her interests went far beyond the local area. She traveled alone to Europe in the 1960s, and reported that one of the highlights of the trip was the time she spent walking from town to town in France, enjoying meeting and living among the local people.

Upon her return to Amherst, she busied herself with helping others, recalling "old times," teaching Sunday School, and driving her little '39 coupe.

and associated activities held there. There were two entrances into the fairgrounds. One was off Hanger Road into the north end of the property. The stables and riding ring were on the left. There were two permanent exhibition buildings—wooden structures painted white, end to end like two boxcars. The rides were south and west of the exhibition buildings. The other entrance came into the east end of the property from West Court Street.

"I lived on Hanger Road, so I was able to crawl through the fence between the fairgrounds and Bud Wright's property. I remember looking at the fresh produce exhibits, canned goods and baked goods (pies were my favorite).

"The rides, costing a nickel or dime, usually consisted of a Ferris wheel, a merry-go-round, swings and rides for smaller kids. There were a

Sallie Hanger, right, and two friends prepare for an afternoon at the fair.
Anne Hanger photo

few games for winning stuffed animals, Chinese handcuffs, and plastic trinkets. I usually only tried the rubber ducks.

"One year there was a ride named the Caterpillar. It went around in a circle on a platform that was wavy. As it picked up speed, a cover folded over the cars placing the rider in the dark, probably a favorite for folks dating. I rode it three times in a row and almost lost my cotton candy on the third session.

"There was talk about one of the swings breaking loose and the rider ending up in a tree. I cannot verify the story, which might have been an early urban legend.

"There were horse shows for Tennessee gaited horses in the riding ring. My uncle Bud Schirmacher always showed his horse there. One of the most fascinating events for me was the jousting tournament. A series of three poles held small rings, and contestants rode the course trying to catch the rings on a lance. The rings became progressively smaller with each round. The winner was whoever snared the most rings. I was amazed anyone could catch those small rings with an eight foot lance while riding a galloping horse!

"A 'Jousting Queen' was named and presented at the much-anticipated tournament dance that night.

"Someone (perhaps the 4-H) sponsored a pet contest. I thought I would take my cat. I was old enough to drive. I caught the cat, put her into a bushel basket with a lid and drove to the fairgrounds. The cat did not like to ride. I took the cat, hissing and clawing inside the basket, to the judges. I proudly popped the lid and reached in, as we all watched that cat making tracks for the fence and the safety of home.

"Large oak trees lined the west side of the property, where the carnival people set up their trailers. Considerable trash was always left behind. I would walk over, place a board against one of the trees and shoot all the glass

bottles and jars with my .22 rifle. One of those trees, if still standing, might have about thirty pounds of lead in it from my bullets and probably five or six inches of broken glass on the ground at the base of the tree. Oh the innocence of youth!"

The current location of Amherst Middle School was called "Gordon's Fairgrounds" before the construction of Central High School in 1956. A large frame building stood on the property; activities such as dances and bingo games were held there. Marianna Penn remembers the baseball games that were an integral

Tommy Littrell's recent drawing of the fairgrounds. Littrell, who lived nearby, spent many hours at the fair. Drawing by Tommy Littrell

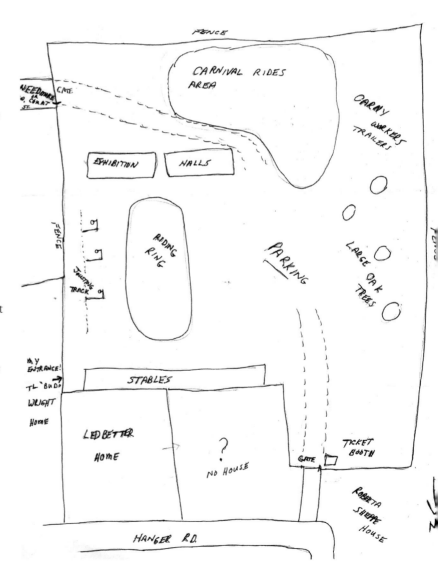

part of the fair. Her husband, Olridge Penn, and James Massie Patteson were managers of baseball teams that played at the fairgrounds.

Charles "Skippy" Brown also recalls that the main feature of the fair held at Gordon's Fairgrounds was baseball, where one of his uncles played. There was much excitement at these games, with teams coming from other areas to challenge the Amherst teams.

The Amherst Fairgrounds property was used for a few other events before it fell quiet forever. Jean Higginbotham remembers a May Day event that the extension service home demonstration club sponsored. She recalls the typical May pole dance, with little girls in nice dresses. There were vendors and exhibits of various types, the details of which have diminished with the years.

Boy Scout meetings were held in one of the fair buildings up until the late '50s or early '60s. Another amusement that occurred on the grounds occasionally was the ever-entertaining "donkey ball game," an event providing a combination of merriment and dust in the air.

These fairs reportedly ceased sometime in the 1950s. Their demise came about as a result of a variety of factors: changes in the use of the property, deteriorating conditions of the structures, less involvement in agriculture, and citizens' greater mobility to entertainment venues in Lynchburg or other areas. ∞

TUBBY WEBSTER

Not everyone who served in the town was born here, though maybe it has seemed that way. The mayor of Amherst in the 1950s was **Frederick Bye "Tubby" Webster**, who came to Amherst through a fairly circuitous route, starting in Montana.

Every knock on the family's front door would leave his mother saying, "What has Fred done now?" When he rode his horse through church as a teen, his parents deemed it advisable to establish some discipline in his life, whereupon they shipped him east to VMI. Philosophical differences between him and the administration over an ethical issue (testifying against a classmate) motivated him to drop out and walk next door to offer his services to play football at Washington and Lee.

A subsequent injury sent him to the hospital, where he was visited by Beverly Randolph Harrison of Amherst, a great fan of W&L football. Harrison brought along his daughter, Frances Ellis Harrison. She soon became Mrs. Frederick Bye Webster and accompanied him back to Montana where he would study law.

They returned to her home in Amherst when he decided law was not his calling. Webster supported his growing family first with railroad work, then in sales with the Esherman Feed Company. They lived at "Edgewood," at the corner of Main and Garland.

118

Flower show at the Amherst County Fair.
Nancy Marion photo

RATTLESNAKE NEVER TASTED SO GOOD

Amherst Boy Scouts have taken full advantage of our county's natural boundaries of ancient mountains and scenic rivers. In the summer of 1958, the troop's leaders planned a survival hike on the Appalachian Trail. The plan was to test our scouting skills to live off the land as we hiked from Crabtree Meadows at the headwaters of the falls southwest to Route 60 on Long Mountain in Amherst County.

We piled into the back of a pickup truck that August morning with no camping or backpacking gear. We had followed our leader Vance Wilkins' instructions to carry only what each of us could cram into a small matchbox. Dick Sandidge carried a razorblade in the hopes of skinning our quarry. Webb Babcock Jr. brought a fishing hook, matches, a rubber band and 10 feet of fishing line. I remember having matches and a large rubber band in hopes of making a slingshot.

Once at Crabtree Meadows, we set forth, looking for the white rectangular blazes marking the Appalachian Trail. We then pretty much left that to Vance while we gave chase to the fastest rabbit in Nelson County for our homemade rotisserie that night.

An hour later, the slingshots had failed miserably. The rabbit had gone to ground. Webb could not find a place to fish and we all resorted to crabapples and blackberries. Dick Sandidge says now he could not look at another blackberry for several years after that.

While in a blackberry patch, I heard what I thought was the jingling of coins in somebody's pocket. That was just before our calm leader informed me, a rather excitable youth, that I had almost stepped on a timber rattler that he now had pinned beneath his walking stick. Vance soon transformed this dreaded creature of the Blue Ridge into what was looking more and more like dinner.

In the meantime, we had lost the trail. Vance directed us toward the Blue Ridge Parkway in the vicinity of Whetstone Ridge. Nightfall found us huddled around an open fire, each with a big glob of rattlesnake on the end of a stick. One lucky marksman had killed a sparrow that when plucked yielded a tasty morsel the size of a dime. Webb Babcock Jr. said it took three days to shake the taste of charred rattlesnake.

The thought of a good home cooked meal inspired us to hit the parkway at a faster pace. We exited at Irish Gap. About midnight under a full moon, we piled together like cordwood, in the words of Vance Wilkins, trying to get warm. It was impossible to sleep. We were on our feet again following the Pedlar River toward Route 60.

Late that morning we made calls home from Forks of Buffalo. Around the family dinner table, I devoured a whole fried chicken and most of a chocolate cake. I can still picture my little brother's incredulous expression as I wove my tale of twenty-four hours in the mountains.

—*Thurman Davis*

119

Service

Jesse Cunningham, often known as "Uncle Jesse," stands near an Amherst Fire Department vehicle when the fire department was located on the south side of Second Street. Visible on each side of Second Street are two hotels, the Belmont (left) and Mays Hotel.
Amherst Fire Department photo

In an earlier article in the Town of Amherst Centennial Series, Robert Wimer noted that one of the first acts of the 1910 Amherst Town Council was to enact a section of ordinances under the general title of "peace, good order and morals." It was designed to maintain order in the town. To that effect, a town sergeant was elected and paid $15.00 per month.

Since that time there have been eleven town sergeants or police chiefs, with Haney "Bobby" Mottley having the longest tenure, serving forty-one years. Chief Mottley (1951–52, 1954–1992) still serves on the Amherst Town Council.

Chief Mottley remembers making $2,700 a year in 1954, with his income supplemented by money collected from the sixty-two parking meters.

Although violent crime has never been a big problem within the town limits, he recalls being deputized by Sheriff Henry Myers to investigate a double homicide in the early 1960s. There he used the investigative skills he learned in the military police with the U.S. Army.

This drama had many of the elements with which we have become too familiar: the matching glove, the pretty thirteen-year-old daughter who was thought to be at school that morning, a failed polygraph test and the accused murderer in his jail cell sobbing that he had not killed the little girl he had affectionately known and called "Baby Doll." Two lives were lost for a paltry sum of money later found hidden on Waugh's Ferry Road.

Police Chief Haney Mottley retired in 1992.

Another experience, not at all violent, but poignant, involved a young indigent who collapsed and died at the Amherst traffic circle. Chief Mottley, through the FBI and Social Security, located his family in Kentucky who requested that their son be buried in decent clothes and receive a dignified service here. This was done at the Poor House Burial Ground on Monitor Road west of Amherst.

Another sad aspect of Mottley's job was dealing with abusive parents since there was no social agency for that purpose then. Fortunately, there were not that many cases, nor was juvenile delinquency a major problem.

However, he recalls the time in the 1960s when several children of prominent Amherst families broke into a local drugstore. They were apprehended with the help of an undercover policeman, posing as a bellhop in Virginia Beach's swankiest hotel, "The Cavalier," where they were spending the loot.

Although drugs started to become a major problem in America in the 1960s, Mottley says they were never a serious issue for the town of Amherst during his tenure.

In the years prior to the Route 29 bypass, thousands of cars in the 1950s and 1960s were funneled through downtown Amherst every day. If anything was amiss, the first responder was the young police chief, in his crisp blue uniform, usually parked on East Court Street facing the traffic as it passed by on Main. A telephone strictly for his use was mounted on a pole located next to his space. If he was out on patrol, the town operator would call someone at the Amherst traffic circle to flag him down at the next passing.

Of course, the "thin blue line" in this country never knows when that next call just might be lethal. Having been called to a large disturbance off Main Street, Mottley was warned by someone in the crowd to take cover from an approaching man carrying a rifle. The chief fired two warning shots into the ground, one on each side of his would-be assailant who then dropped his weapon.

Once when making an arrest of an unruly character in the courthouse yard, a scuffle ensued resulting in a black eye for Mottley. Another call came from Central Fidelity on South Main when a bank robber had already put the town limits far behind him. The chief today is so thankful that in all those experiences he never had to fire his .38-caliber pistol at anyone.

The chief spent nearly four hours in the municipal building, recalling some of these events that helped define his life and the town of Amherst. We walked out beneath the portrait given in his honor by a grateful Town Council. As we crossed Main Street on a rainy January night, I followed him to his car parked in that same spot either out of habit or nostalgia where a much younger "Bobby" Mottley, as we affectionately called him, could usually be found on call for the town. Because of his service and those who have followed him, Amherst is a safer and a better place.

Amherst town sergeants and police chiefs: Walker Gregory, Chester Coffey, C. W. Campbell, Robert Miller, John Beard, Maurice Gannaway Sr., S. H. Grogan Jr., L. H. Dalton, Haney Mottley, Mahlon Bryant, Kenneth Watts.

—*Thurman Davis*

FIRE DEPARTMENT BORN OF NECESSITY

By Patty Walton Turpin

The Amherst Fire Department was born of a disaster in 1917 when a fire destroyed three prominent businesses: the Amherst Livery Stable, the old Meeks building and the Hill Hardware lumber yard. With no firefighting personnel or equipment, the property was a loss. Five years before that event, another devastating fire had destroyed several buildings in the town. The only help available was through a group of men forming a bucket brigade.

Jesse Cunningham, an Amherst resident who was a thirty-year veteran with the Hampton Fire Department, then organized a fire department with five other men: John Beard, Rector Hunt, Walker Gregory, Joe Goodwin, and John Shrader.

The first fire truck was an American La France horse-drawn chemical engine, used until 1920 when a motorized Stewart truck was acquired. In 1927, a new Chevy chassis was obtained and firemen built the engine themselves. In 1932, a wrecked Model A Ford was built into a firefighting vehicle, which the members called the "Jeep." In 1942 a Dodge fire truck was used and could pump 600 gallons a minute.

Fred Loving, firefighter and historian of the department, indicates that the first fire house was built in 1926 on Main Street next to the current town hall. The department then moved to a new station on Second Street near the

123

Some of Amherst Fire Department's founding members, with their firefighting vehicle in front of the Farmers Bank of Amherst From left, unidentified, Edloe Shanks, (standing on truck) John Shrader, Tom Hatcher, James E. Bowman, banker; Jesse Cunningham at the wheel, Billy Sandidge, and Rector Hunt.
Paul Wailes III photo

Right: Fire truck in front of the Amherst Fire Department headquarters on the south side of Second Street.
Amherst Fire Department photo

present Amherst newspaper office. The present fire house, erected in 1963 and enlarged in 1995, now stands across Second Street from its previous location.

To notify the department of a fire in progress, three fire alarm boxes were installed around town. The telephone operator was able to set off two sirens which could be heard for a distance of seven miles. In 1952, the Gulf Station at the traffic circle took the calls. Today, the 911 system has been employed and the alarm still sounds when a fire has been reported.

Funding for the fire department, as for any public service, was difficult to obtain. In the early days, the founders realized that their fund raisers such as bingo games and dances were not generating enough money.

Billy Sandidge appealed to the Town Council for funds in 1928 to no avail. Sandidge returned with a petition promoting an auto license fee. This petition led to a required auto tag in Amherst, thereby providing financial support for the fire department.

Following is a summary of memorable fires in the department's history:

1927: Scott house on Garland Avenue.

1930: Sweet Briar House.

1930: Dr. Dayton Watts home, Christmas Day.

1944: Leith house (current location of Fairmont Crossing); lightning strike.

1947: G&T Restaurant, in the Allen building, corner of Main and East Court streets.

1948: Amherst Milling. This fire may have started near a diesel engine. Vance Wilkins remembers running down from school to help. After the fire had been extinguished, he was asked to crawl into the grain chute to find potential "hot spots." As a twelve-year-old, he was the smallest person available.

1951: Main Street fire.

The retired fire chief, Jesse Cunningham, universally known as "Uncle Jesse," was almost

The Amherst Fire Department responded to a major fire on Main Street in 1951.
The News & Advance photo

overcome by smoke in his apartment in the Coffee Shop building. He heard the crackling noise of flames and reported the fire. Cunningham narrowly escaped being pinned by the collapse of the roof. Wood's Grocery, the Western Auto, and a dance hall were destroyed.

It had been a dry summer and the firemen were unable to draw enough water from the hydrants in the town's system. Chief Edloe Shanks ordered the town's pumps out of action to improve the flow to the fire. A double wall on the north side of the building stopped the fire from spreading.

Some firefighters were nearly trapped when a roof collapsed. Ed Ware was saved by his helmet when a gutter fell. John Shrader was cut by glass.

Fire trucks from Monelison, Gladstone, and Piney River also assisted.

1955: Downtown Lynchburg fire. The Amherst Fire Department was on stand-by to assist the Lynchburg Fire Department.

1963: A record-setting year for forest fires in Central Virginia.

1964: C&C Tire Company. An old building at the current location of Amherst Publishing Company, formerly housing a car dealership, was being used by J. C. and George Cash for tire recapping. The floors saturated by oil and

L. John Denney, mayor, Dorothy Dickey, council member, and Larry Littrell, town manager, converse in front of Burch and Ogden in the 1970s.
Amherst County Historical Museum photo

grease, along with tires and recapping materials, provided a perfect medium for a rapid and hot fire.

Even with the fire department directly across the street, the business was destroyed. Also engulfed were several cars, some owned by the telephone company. The fire department's job became protecting nearby buildings, the town hall, and library.

Equipment, training, and support have evolved over the almost one century of the department's existence, with the Amherst County Department of Public Safety tying in the 911 system in recent years. Current vehicles include three pumpers, one tanker, a ladder truck, and a brush truck; also housed is an antique 1946 Dodge fire truck.

Both the Town of Amherst and Amherst

When telephone service was considered a luxury by some, residents resorted to communication the old fashioned way. Such was the modus operandi of Pierce Massie and Kinckle Allen, two attorneys with upstairs offices on opposite sides of Main Street. When one wanted the other, he would just raise his window and holler across for the other lawyer to step to his window.

PIERCE MASSIE & KINCKLE ALLEN

Attorney Kinckle Allen

County help finance the department's needs, including workmen's compensation and vehicle insurance costs.

A milestone of vital significance is the availability now of an SCBA (self-contained breathing apparatus) for each firefighter. In the 1960s, members shared such equipment, severely limiting their ability to perform particular tasks.

Firefighters train through in-house coursework as well as participation in activities through the Central Virginia Fire Training

facility. At this venue, firefighters can experience live-action situations.

Professional emergency medical technicians are now financed by the county through the rescue squads. These EMTs all hold at least Firefighter 1 status, as well.

In firefighting, response time is paramount. Communication has evolved dramatically, from the days of interrupting party-line telephone conversations to report a fire, to the current instant notification of all firefighters through a personal radio system.

Within the past decade, equipment improvements also include the acquisition of a ladder truck, financed in part by the Town of Amherst, Sweet Briar College, and Greif Brothers. Not only is this equipment vital to saving lives and property, but its availability has had significant impact on fire insurance costs for local businesses.

The Amherst Fire Department currently has a volunteer staff of 27 members, each serving one weekend a month at the station. Members speak of the close relationships and camaraderie that are natural outcomes of their cooperative efforts in firefighting.

Often it is a family affair. Three generations of the Shrader family have been with the department, amassing more than 150 years of combined service. Fire Chiefs Cunningham, Shanks, Patteson, and Wydner all served for more than two decades each.

Although not a large organization, the fire department and its dedicated members provide an invaluable service to the town and surrounding area—a significant benefit coming from the unfortunate events of 1917.

Amherst Fire Chiefs: Jesse Cunningham, Edloe Shanks, C. S. "Peck" Patteson, William Wydner, Walter Turner, Trent Ritchie, Tom Shrader. ∞

MUTT AND THE JUDGE

In the 1940s, a stray dog followed Gordon Dearborn home north of the traffic circle one day. The children loved him and named him Mutt. Every day he would walk to the bank uptown and sleep under Dearborn's desk. Any time Judge Edward Meeks saw the dog in daily commute, the judge would stop and give Mutt a ride to the bank.

Judge Edward Meeks

Farrar Saunders, who worked at Amherst Publishing Company behind the courthouse, sits at the wheel of one the old fire engines.
Alvin Womack photo

NO. 1.

Right: Amherst Life Saving Crew's early vehicles in the 1960s.
Amherst County Historical Museum photo

Below: John McKee, representing Diuguid Funeral Home, presents an old hearse to the Amherst Lifesaving Crew members, from left, Harry Wilkerson, Radford Brent, Wendell Burford, Yale Burch, J. C. Cash, Gilbert Cash, and George Roe.
Amherst Life Saving Crew photo

FIRST RESCUE VEHICLE
WAS AN OLD HEARSE

By Patty Walton Turpin

"Humble beginnings" surely would describe the Amherst Life Saving Crew's formative years—from Red Cross first aid classes being taught on the steps of the health building (because somebody forgot to unlock the building) to an old hearse converted into a rescue vehicle.

The need for a life saving crew in Amherst became obvious in the 1950s when emergency transportation for victims of an automobile accident was delayed. A Lynchburg funeral home that would send an ambulance demanded payment first, because those involved were from out of state.

There had been an attempt to develop a rescue squad in 1957, but it never came to fruition. This group had been given an old hearse, which was stored in the Health Department basement. Seeking a doctor or using the private ambulance service continued to be the only options, although sometimes Haney Mottley, the town police officer, was available to respond to medical emergencies and transport a victim to the hospital.

In 1958 a group of Amherst men—Harry Wilkerson, Millard Godwin, George Roe, Donald Mays, Wendell Burford, Hugh Garbee, Yale Burch, Ronald Shrader, and J. C. Cash, under the leadership of Mottley—laid the groundwork for development of a life saving crew. The actual founding date for the organization is 1959, when basic and advanced first aid certifications were completed by the prospective members.

Diuguid Funeral Home donated an additional hearse to be converted into an ambulance. A 1958 Ford was purchased from Julian Harris for the creation of a crash truck. This work was provided by Harry Wilkerson. Funds were raised to outfit the ambulance and crash truck. In September 1959, the Amherst Life Saving and First Aid crew was ready to respond to emergency medical calls. Barnes Brockman of Amherst Ford later provided a 1962 Ford ambulance.

The first location for the ALSC was the present Hill House. Later it expanded into Wilkerson's auto body shop in the lower section of the same building.

In the 1980s, under the leadership of Captain Sandra Chandler and Treasurer Gil Tracey, the life saving crew raised funds for a larger and more efficient building. Individuals, businesses, and companies donated windows, entire rooms and equipment, enabling the organization to move into its headquarters debt-free in 1987. The crew continues to operate out of this building, which is located just east of the traffic circle on Route 60.

Life saving crew members helped with organizing Gladstone, Pedlar, Monelison and Roseland rescue squads. Having life saving crews located in other areas of the county greatly enhanced each unit's ability to respond quickly and effectively.

The squad has maintained high standards in acquiring the most up-to-date equipment avail-

Amherst Life Saving Crew assisted in search and rescue efforts following Hurricane Camille in August, 1969.
Amherst Life Saving Crew photo

able. Their box unit gave crew members more room to perform emergency treatment. It was the first rural crew in the area to receive the "jaws of life," which helped dramatically in extricating passengers in automobile accidents. This device was given in 1972, in memory of Donald Selvage Sr. The crew was the second in the state to elect a woman captain, Becky Parr Bryant. It was also the first crew in Central Virginia to use AST (anti-shock trousers), which had been developed by the military for use in Vietnam.

In the 1970s, advanced life support systems were implemented, enabling rescue personnel to communicate directly with the hospital from the field: monitoring blood pressure, pulse, and oxygen saturation, sending EKGs, starting IVs, administering drugs, defibrillating patients. This equipment is routine today, but was "cutting edge," especially in rural areas, at that time. All vehicles are now equipped with these capabilities. Specialized equipment, such as a stair chair, a battery-powered stretcher that lifts, and a heavy-duty stretcher, enable responders to negotiate a variety of situations they may face.

In its half-century of service, the Amherst Life Saving Crew has answered thousands of calls, some of historic proportions.

On August 19–20, 1969, Hurricane Camille unleashed its fury on Nelson County with a world-record torrent of water, measured by some at more than thirty inches in a five-hour period. The ALSC assisted with search and rescue. Brothers John and Al Turner, along with Warren Campbell, junior members at the time, served on a Marine helicopter with Sheriff Bill Whitehead of Nelson County. The pilot of the helicopter was a Vietnam veteran who was adept at maneuvering through the mountainous terrain. One of their first assignments was to go into isolated areas to evacuate survivors. They later took recovered bodies to local funeral homes.

A call on Oct. 6, 1982, resulted in a bit of confusion in communicating the nature of the scene: a U-Haul truck's load had shifted on Madison Heights hill, overturning and pinning an oncoming Volkswagen "Beetle." When life saving crews quickly arrived and assessed the situation, they found that the load was 64 University of Virginia Sigma Chi members on a road-trip to Randolph-Macon Woman's College.

Some squads had interpreted the information to possibly involve a bus going down a ravine. The Amherst Life Saving Crew answered and had brought a 4-wheel drive vehicle for potentially rough terrain. The crew stabilized, treated, and transported many of the sixty-six victims to the Lynchburg General Hospital Emergency Room. The final tally from this tragedy was two fatalities, several severe brain injuries, and numerous lives forever altered by the events of that October night.

Later in the 1980s, the squad responded to the Southern Crescent train accident in Nelson County. Access to the train was gained by a narrow road or path requiring the rescue vehicles to back up for three quarters of a mile. They transported several passengers to the hospital.

Members can fulfill a variety of roles. Some are drivers only; they must be at least 21 years old to be certified as drivers. Emergency medical technicians advance through various phases of training, assuming greater responsibilities at each level.

Junior members, starting at age 16, can explore opportunities to experience life as a rescue worker, building a strong foundation for future careers. The Amherst Life Saving Crew has launched several former junior members into related careers in medical and rescue work. Those in emergency services in Lynchburg include Paul Kilgore, a battalion chief; his son Joey Kilgore, firefighter EMT; Sam Bryant, captain and EMS supervisor; Jason Campbell, captain; and Frankie Campbell, captain; Mark Whiting, senior regional director with the American Red Cross in Richmond; Danny Fell, owner of a medical supply company; Charlie Rucker, lieutenant with Roanoke County Fire Department; and Sandra Garrette, a registered nurse in Charlottesville.

Today, in addition to responding to other emergency calls, the forty members of the crew are called upon to do stand-by duty for local events: festivals, sports, graduations, Relay for Life, and 5K walks. Glenda Hash is the current captain. Two professional EMTs work Monday through Friday, 7 a.m. to 5 p.m., with volunteers covering the rest of the hours each day. Volunteers work ninety-six hours a month and rotate weekends as well. The unit has four advanced life support ambulances, one medium-duty rescue truck, and a first-response utility vehicle.

Those doing rescue work recognize valuable life lessons as they advance through training and gain experience: teamwork, responsibility, communication, decision-making, and performing in pressure situations. Members make lasting friendships while helping their community. The benefit to the town is beyond measure. The founding members are to be lauded for their foresight and perseverance. ∞

Below left: Florence Yancey and her son, Bill, at the time of her 100th birthday.

Below: Florence Yancey, born in 1870, as a young woman.
Marianna Penn photos

"SIS" YANCEY

The Amherst citizen who probably enjoyed the greatest longevity was **Florence Yancey**, affectionately known as "Sis" or "Aunt Florence." Not only did she live to age 107, but she also left a legacy stretching several generations through her work as a certified midwife.

During her half-century of service with a half dozen local doctors, as well as on her own, she estimated the number of deliveries at 500, as stated in an interview at the time of her retirement in 1956. Her work took her to remote locations with only the rudimentary accoutrements for delivering babies—candlelight at best, and often no running water.

When asked about any fears she may have had in her late-night travels to remote areas, she covered all contingencies, "I have always lived with God and a gun."

The most notable accessory to her countenance even late in life was a corncob pipe. She herself was the mother of nine children, and has numerous descendants still in Amherst.

SENATOR WARNER
TIED CLOSELY WITH AMHERST

By Thurman B. Davis

On the occasion of the town's centennial, former U.S. Sen. John Warner recalled his Amherst heritage with a tone of warmth, affection and gratitude for this historic community. His grandfather came to Amherst from Maryland shortly after the Civil War. What prompted his coming is not known, but the move was providential because he met and married Mary Tinsley whose family had been in Amherst since the 1700s.

A stained glass window at Ascension Church in Amherst honors the Rev. Charles Tinsley Warner, an Episcopal minister born in Amherst. He left to become rector for forty years at St. Albans Church in Washington, D.C.

It was his wish to be buried in Amherst and his tombstone, featuring a Christian cross, lies only twenty feet from an identical marker for his lifetime friend Walter Harrison Carter.

Charles Warner (1877–1949) and his brother John (1883–1946), father of Sen. Warner, were longtime friends of Carter, an Amherst native who practiced law, served as a senator in the General Assembly, and lived in a stately home on Garland Avenue.

Sen. Warner's grandfather practiced law in Amherst and shortly after the birth of their first son, Mrs. Warner developed arthritis, prompting the family's move to Rockville, Md., where she received special medical care.

Warner's father was born there in 1883 and, for the rest of his life, would lament that he had not been "born a Virginian." Through the years, the Warner brothers remained close both to their Tinsley roots and to Sen. Carter.

The Tinsley family encouraged Sen. Warner's father to go to Washington and Lee, where he excelled in the classics, graduating with honors in 1903. With his love of Greek and Latin, he became headmaster of a one-room academy for boys near Winchester, where he boarded with a doctor's family. To pay for his room and board he drove the doctor's "Model T" and often assisted the doctor as he tended to patients.

After several years, the doctor said: "You have learned a lot about medicine, so now is the time for you to get further training." He won a scholarship to New York University Medical College.

Sadly, some of his earliest patients were fellow soldiers, as the young doctor volunteered for the Army in World War I, with service in the trenches in France in 1917–18.

Although the Warner brothers were in Washington, they often visited Amherst where they had a sizeable tract of land inherited from their parents. Walter Carter handled the property and arranged for the cutting of timber to pay the taxes.

An amused Sen. Warner recalled in a telephone conversation a story about a time the two brothers were walking over the land with Carter when they detected a peculiar scent emanating from the woods. Carter, wise to the custom of "moonshining" in the county, had to physically restrain the decorous Episcopal rector who became incensed that someone dared to conduct such nefarious operations "on my land!" Upon Carter's orders the brothers made a swift departure from their woods rather than assault the still.

The senator as a youngster accompanied his father and uncle on trips to Amherst County and he, too, took pride in his Virginia roots. In the family tradition of military service, he volunteered at 17 and served in the Navy in the last year of World War II.

Within months of his honorable discharge, Warner enrolled at Washington and Lee University. He recalled with poignant clarity the long line, stretching from the Lee Chapel to the Colonnade, of young veteran enrollees, some still wearing bits of military garb as civilian clothes were scarce. But they were "armed" with the World War II G.I. Bill, one of America's finest investments.

In that first year at Washington and Lee, Walter Carter solemnly came to Warner's classroom one day, beckoned to him, and told him that his father, a prominent physician in Washington, had just died. Carter drove the young student across the mountain and arranged for him to catch a bus to Washington, D.C., for the funeral conducted at St. Albans Church by his uncle.

His remaining years at W&L, the senator

recalled, involved serious study but there were carefree trips over the mountains to Sweet Briar where "we were always gentlemen." On late or foggy nights, he often stayed overnight at Walter Carter's home rather than drive that winding road back to Lexington.

He often took his dates to Ye Olde Travelers Coffee Shop. Beer was the drink of choice and, if patrons became raucous, "Mama George" Tsoleas would literally take the unruly offender by the collar and lead him "firmly" outside. Years later when Warner returned to Amherst to campaign for the Senate, he sent a driver for Mrs. Tsoleas so she could attend the rally on the courthouse steps.

After receiving a degree in basic engineering, Warner was uncertain about his future. Once again Walter Carter's influence prevailed. Warner

Former U.S. Sen. John Warner

U.S. Senator John Warner's ancestors came from Amherst County. He spent considerable time in town in his early years.

recalls spending several days at Carter's home in the summer of 1949, and, on the side porch, the longtime friend and confidant told the young W&L graduate that he thought law school at the university would be wise. Carter, a lawyer himself, signed the application papers and John Warner entered the University of Virginia Law School in the fall of 1949.

His law studies were interrupted by a second tour of active military service as he volunteered for the U.S. Marine Corps during the Korean War. Upon returning from duty

133

Carter Glass, a widower from Lynchburg, former U.S. Congressman and Senator, Secretary of the Treasury under Woodrow Wilson, and founder of the Federal Reserve System, married Amherst resident **Mary Scott Meade**, a widow and Latin and English teacher at Amherst School. Her students at the high school were always fascinated by the arrival on Friday afternoon of a limousine for Mrs. Meade. Although the wedding ceremony was small, with Senator **Harry F. Byrd Sr.** as the sole out-of-town guest, the students found out the date and time of the wedding and heartily cheered the newlyweds as they emerged from the Ascension Church in June 1940.

L. F. PAYNE SR.

Directing traffic in Williamsburg provided **L. F. Payne Sr.** with the opportunity to meet the attractive young woman in the car beside him. Thus was the beginning of the union that brought L. F. and Dolly

Payne to Amherst, where he had been assigned with the Virginia State Police in 1940.

His piercing eyes, starched uniform, and shiny belt buckle belied his nickname of "Easy" that was based on a quiet manner, soft voice and dry sense of humor.

He was a great teller of stories, recounting experiences of drunkards in fights, tragic automobile accidents, truck fires, thefts, and an occasional murder. His knack for solving problems and helping others in difficult circumstances earned him respect and many personal letters filled with gratitude for good deeds.

Being part of several high profile murder investigations brought Trooper Payne acclaim from newspaper and national magazine coverage. His careful investigations and clear accounts of what happened earned him high marks in the courts and success with convictions of people with serious offenses. Nevertheless he maintained a demeanor reflecting quiet humility.

Virginia State Trooper L.F. Payne Sr. in 1941.
Mary Ball Payne Morton photo

with the First Marine Air Wing in Korea, as a first lieutenant, he returned to U.Va. and finished law school.

He became a law clerk to a federal judge, then an assistant U.S. Attorney followed by a period of private practice. He returned to public service as Secretary of the Navy (1969–1974) in the Nixon-Ford administration. He later was appointed director of the American Revolution Bicentennial Administration, under President Ford, which administered federal programs honoring the Founding Fathers.

In 1978, Warner won election to the U.S. Senate from Virginia, was re-elected four consecutive times, and eventually became chairman of the powerful Senate Armed Services Committee. This post served Virginia well since the state is one of the top four states in receiving sources of funding for national defense.

He recalled with a sense of irony that, at age fourteen, he first experienced the political scene in Virginia when his uncle Charles took him to a campaign rally outside Winchester. A large crowd had gathered to hear Sen. Harry Byrd Sr. As if on cue, the senator, in his crisp white linen suit, walked among the mesmerized crowd (many in bib overalls) and railed—in a strong speech delivered from the back of an orchard truck—against wasteful federal spending in Washington.

Little did the youthful Warner dream that someday he would serve thirty years in that august body, passing the twenty-nine-year record of Sen. Carter Glass, of Lynchburg, and becoming the second-longest serving U.S. Senator from Virginia. Harry Byrd Sr. remains the longest with thirty-two years.

Warner attributes his longevity and that of his predecessors to "the fine spring water flowing in Lynchburg, Amherst and Winchester, (which) enabled the three senators to set these extraordinary records of service … to Virginia." ∞

SON OF AMHERST
GOES TO WASHINGTON

By James D. Settle

Former U.S. Sen. John Warner, who spoke at Amherst's Centennial observance on April 17, 2010, has a number of ties with the town and its people. The individual who introduced him—former Congressman L. F. Payne Jr.—is a son of Amherst itself.

Born in 1945 to State Police officer L. F. Payne and his wife Dolly, a teacher in Amherst for many years, the younger Payne graduated from Amherst County High School in 1963 and received his bachelor's degree in Civil Engineering from the Virginia Military Institute in 1967.

Six years later, after active duty in the U.S. Army, Payne earned an MBA from the University of Virginia's Darden School of Business. He and his firm were instrumental in the development of the Wintergreen Resort in Nelson County.

After a number of years of involvement in politics, he was chosen by special election in 1988 to succeed the late Congressman W. C. "Dan" Daniel in representing the Fifth Virginia Congressional District. He was reelected several times, serving until 1997, when he resigned to involve himself more closely in statewide politics.

For the last dozen years, he has worked in government relations with the Washington firm, McGuire Woods Consulting.

He and his wife Susan live in Charlottesville and are the parents of four children.

L. F. Payne Jr.

As do others who graduated from the schools and participated in other facets of Amherst life, such as church, youth sports, and Boy Scouts, Payne has fond memories of his time in the town, noting wryly that his political career benefited from his family's local involvement. He recalled one person commenting to him on the campaign trail, "I'm voting for you because your mother taught me in school."

Although his congressional district did not include Amherst, and his current schedule requires considerable time spent in travel, he still enjoys returning to the scenes and people of his early life. He noted that he especially looked forward to introducing Sen. Warner to his own hometown on the occasion of the Centennial of the incorporation of the Town of Amherst. ∞

TOWN WELL REPRESENTED IN RICHMOND OVER THE YEARS

By Robert C. Wimer

Lucian Shrader
The News & Advance
photo

The funeral train of President **Franklin Delano Roosevelt** passed through Amherst in the early hours of April 14, 1945.

In its first 100 years, the town of Amherst has had its share of leaders elected to the Virginia General Assembly. Those men, beginning with former Judge Clarence J. Campbell who served in the House of Delegates in 1922 and 1923, and concluding with S. Vance Wilkins Jr., who rose to the pinnacle of power in the state legislature as Speaker of the House in 2000, ensured that Amherst and the voice of Virginia's rural localities was heard in Richmond.

Lucian H. Shrader followed a few years after Del. Campbell having been first elected to the House of Delegates in 1925. He served continuously until 1939. Shrader, who died in 1976 at the age of 82, had an active and successful career as an attorney, judge, businessman and legislator.

He attended public schools in Amherst and the University of Virginia, where he received his law degree. He was admitted to the bar in 1918 and began practicing law in Amherst County.

The young lawyer was the first Army enlistee from Amherst County during World War I, having enlisted in Charlot-tesville. He served with the University Ambulance Unit during the war.

Shrader's interest in law and journalism (he and his wife purchased the *Amherst New Era-Progress* in 1920 and published it and several other weekly newspapers until 1946) soon extended to politics. A lifelong Democrat, he was first elected to the House in 1925 and served until 1939, when he resigned to accept appointment as Amherst County trial justice. In 1950, he also became Juvenile and Domestic Relations judge, a position he filled until 1964.

Shrader gave some fleeting thought to running for governor in 1949, declaring himself a candidate for the Democratic primary that year. He withdrew from the contest before becoming actively involved.

Many folks growing up in Amherst during his tenure as judge from 1940 to 1973 would be confronted by him in the courthouse for one infraction or another. Usually, it was a traffic offense for which a stern lecture was delivered along with the guilty verdict.

Judge Shrader stepped down from the bench in July 1973 at the age of 70.

Sen. I. Paul Wailes

Former state Sen. I. Paul Wailes, who lived on Garland Avenue, once told a reporter that his first campaign for the seat representing Amherst, Bedford and Nelson counties was long and hard. He was running against four opponents and said, "Five people—that made for a right interesting campaign."

The campaigns never got any easier for the traveling shoe salesman who turned politician. Although he was born in Nelson County, he spent most of his life in Amherst, which he represented in the Senate from 1940 to 1952.

He lost his first bid for the Democratic nomination for the Senate seat in the 1935 primary by 31 votes. But that was enough to whet his appetite for politics, according to his son, Paul Wailes III. "When he found out what he lost by, his hat was in the ring for the next time," said the younger Wailes.

Wailes was a Democrat, but took the view that the candidate was more important than the party when it came to casting one's ballot. He was perhaps best remembered among Virginia Democrats for splitting with President Truman and the Democratic Party in 1948 to support Strom Thurmond and the Dixiecrats. He campaigned hard for the "state's rights Democrats" in that presidential election. He referred to the state's rights ticket as "reorganizers of a disintegrated national Democratic Party."

During his years in the Senate, he was appointed to the Finance, and Privileges and Elections committees, two of the body's most powerful.

Wailes once estimated he was paid $12 a day for his position as a state senator and said he retired from politics for financial reasons. "I was afraid I'd end up a pauper if I didn't get back to my personal business," he told a reporter.

He died in 1986 at the age of 89.

Sen. Walter H. Carter

Democrats in the Fourth Senatorial District didn't have to go far to find an Amherst successor to Sen. Wailes. Walter H. Carter lived just up the street from Wailes on Garland Avenue. Carter was elected in 1952 and served for one term until 1956, when he was confronted by a new senate district that had been redrawn as a result of the 1950 census. The new 11th District was the largest in the state, including, in addition to Amherst, the counties of Appomattox, Buckingham, Cumberland, Powhatan, Nelson and Amelia.

Carter said he did not believe he could give sufficient time to his law practice to attend to the business of the larger district.

Before his election to the Senate, Carter, who received his education at Washington and Lee University, had a long and distinguished political career in Amherst. He was treasurer of Amherst County from 1922 to 1924 and mayor of the town from 1928 to 1931.

In 1932, he was elected commonwealth's attorney of Amherst County, a position he held for 20 years before being elected to the Virginia Senate. He served as an infantryman during World War I.

Early in 1965, J. B. Wyckoff joined Carter as a partner in a new law firm. In September of that year, Carter died in a Richmond hospital. He was 75.

Several weeks after his death, business in Amherst County Circuit Court, where Carter had spent many years prosecuting those who ran afoul of the law in Amherst, stopped briefly for a memorial service in his honor. It was led by the Rev. Bailey F. Davis, pastor of Amherst Baptist Church, where Carter had been a life-long member.

Paul Wailes
The News & Advance
photo

Walter Carter
The News & Advance
photo

Future President Richard Nixon accompanied his daughter to Sweet Briar College in the early 1960s when she was touring prospective colleges.

Del. Donald G. Pendleton

"Politics is the art of the possible," Del. Donald G. Pendleton of Amherst used to tell those interested in the General Assembly and the legislative process. He was a skilled politician who played the legislative process like a finely tuned violin. He won as many battles as he lost.

Pendleton, a lawyer by trade, and a Democrat, was first elected to the House from Amherst by a 15-vote margin in 1965. That earned him his first nickname in the legislature—"Landslide." His re-election in 1967 confirmed the moniker, as he won again by a whisker-thin margin of 65 votes.

The lawmaker spent 12 years in the House of Delegates, rising to chairman of the House Committee on Health, Welfare and Institutions, an influential position.

His second nickname? That was "Rooster," which came as a result of his spirited advocacy of the issue of the day. Former state Sen. Elliot S. Schewel of Lynchburg described Pendleton as a "very colorful individual," and added, "He also was quite a fighter for what he thought was

Don Pendleton
The News & Advance
photo

right, and he reminded some of his colleagues of a bantam rooster."

Pendleton was a graduate of Lynchburg College and the University of Virginia Law School. While he was not attending to his legislative duties, he practiced law in Amherst for 32 years. He was a veteran of the U.S. Army and served on active duty in Korea with the 82nd Airborne Division. He retired as a lieutenant colonel in the Virginia National Guard.

In the spring of 1977, Pendleton may have sensed it was time to step down. He announced he would not run for re-election, but was eventually drafted for a seventh term. He lost that

BILLY SANDIDGE

One of the most iconic figures in Amherst was the late William E. "Billy" Sandidge, clerk of the Amherst Circuit Court from 1933 to 1984. His father and grandfather had also held that same position. Anyone who lived in Amherst during those years remembers the quintessential Virginia gentleman walking from his home on south Main Street to open his office at the courthouse promptly at 6:45 every morning.

He cut an imposing figure, tall, perfectly erect and always in an immaculate dark suit. His son Dick said that when his father descended the staircase early in the morning he was already in his suit. When he returned late that evening, the suit stayed on through dinner, a practice he perpetuated long after retirement.

But he was also a man who loved the outdoors and found time to hunt quail behind his two English Setters. With his 16-gauge, double barrel shotgun, he brought many a bird to the dinner table. He also loved to fish and water-ski even into his mid-eighties. When he died in 2005 at the age of 101, many people remembered him as a local man with deep Amherst County roots. He also wielded real power within the Virginia Democratic Party and was host to many of the state's political leaders in his gracious home on South Main Street.

year—in a five-way race for two seats in the district that included Amherst and Lynchburg.

S. Vance Wilkins Jr., a Republican who had barely lost to Pendleton in a couple of earlier races, beat him that year.

Like those who preceded him, Donald G. Pendleton was a landmark in Central Virginia politics. He was faithful to his party and to those he represented—and not just those who voted for him. And in his legal career, he earned the deep and abiding respect of lawyers and judges alike.

A heart attack claimed the feisty lawmaker at the age of 63 in 1995.

Del. S. Vance Wilkins Jr.

The election of S. Vance Wilkins Jr. to the House of Delegates in 1977 ensured that an Amherst resident would retain one of the two seats in the House district. After running several times unsuccessfully, Wilkins, a Republican, finished ahead of his old rival, Del. Donald G. Pendleton.

Wilkins, now 74 and retired from his construction business and politics, would go on to win re-election to 11 additional terms, having served from 1978 to 2002. In 2000, he became the first non-Democratic Speaker of the House since the early 1880s.

A graduate of Virginia Tech, the former lawmaker served in the U.S. Air Force from 1958 to 1960. After returning to Amherst from the Air Force, he became interested in politics, especially Republican politics. In those days in Amherst, the Republican Party could meet in a phone booth.

In 1962, he ran unsuccessfully for a seat on the Amherst County Board of Supervisors against J. B. McDearmon, the newspaper publisher whose experience on the board was difficult to beat. Wilkins said in an interview he did not expect to win the contest, but he wanted to provide some competition in the election.

After observing the election of Democrat John O. Marsh to Congress over J. Kenneth Robinson, the Republican, in the early 1960s, Wilkins said he saw a need to work among Republicans throughout the state to get more of them elected to public office.

The Amherst resident has been credited with being the driving force in the expansion of Republican House membership in the 1980s and 1990s, especially after he became minority leader in 1992. In his first term as Speaker, he oversaw the redistricting of the House after the 2000 census that led to an increase of the Republican majority from 52–47 with one independent to 64–34 with two independents after the November 2001 election.

Wilkins' tenure as Speaker ended with his resignation in June 2002.

Wilkins believes that his greatest political achievement was "to help create a politically competitive environment in the Commonwealth of Virginia." A number of his colleagues in Richmond and elsewhere around the state would agree with that.

Commenting on his experiences growing up in Amherst, he said, "I don't know how it could have been any better." ∞

Vance Wilkins
The News & Advance photo

MISS VERA

Vera Joyner, known by all as "Miss Vera," hired by the elder William Sandidge as deputy court clerk in the early years of the century, continued through the tenure of the succeeding clerk Sandidge, and became an indispensable source of information and direction to every lawyer practicing in Amherst.

Her physical infirmity—a critical curvature of the spine—did not deter her from maintaining an encyclopedic knowledge of case files, dispositions, and chronological data of births, marriages, deaths, wills, and deeds—as well as the work required behind a typewriter with the extra-long carriage to accommodate oversized legal documents.

Many young attorneys, thinking they were savvy to the minutiae of a given case or procedure, would recall Miss Vera's admonition, "No, that's not the way it is—you need to look under ..."

Miss Vera could be seen in town almost daily, as she walked from her home on Main Street, north of the circle. A newspaper feature written in 1950 described her as "a sprightly little woman, who has a cheerful word for everyone she sees."

Miss Vera Joyner
Dorothy Kent Harvey photo

139

Aerial view of Amherst around 2005.
Town of Amherst photo

In Our Time

AMHERST HOME INVESTMENT Co.

OFFICERS:

President— S. BRANCH WALKER, Esq., Walker's Ford, Va.

Secretary and Treasurer— HOUSTON C. JOYNER, Esq. (Treasurer of Amherst County)

Attorneys { JNO. L. LEE, (Commonwealth's Attorney of Amherst County,)
William T. VOORHEIS, of Amherst, Va.

DIRECTORS:

S. BRANCH WALKER,   Hon. WM. DILLARD,   JNO. L. LEE,
HOUSTON C. JOYNER,   WM. T. VOORHEIS

1891

Scale 50 Feet to an Inch

M. H. Garland C. E.

This 1891 plat shows the plans for a large development for property south of downtown Amherst. The development never became reality. Main Street is shown, as well as the faint drawing of Ascension Episcopal with steeple, the Robertson house, Edgewood, and the Jack Lee house. It is printed on cloth and is currently in the Paul Wailes collection.

LIFE IN A FASTER LANE

By James D. Settle

Most of the preceding profiles of Amherst, or Amherst Court House as it was known by some of the "old timers," and its people have described its setting as a small, generally tranquil, rural town—essentially the center of its residents' attention and activities. By the 1970s, though, Amherst, like innumerable American "burgs," was becoming part of a larger canvas, for its own people as well as for others. There is very little that is "self-contained" now—what happened, and when?

Employment patterns changed. The early 1930s opening of the American Cyanamid plant in Piney River was thought to be a good omen. Well-paying, steady jobs in the Depression era were a Godsend. Scientists and professionals moved into the area. As the years passed, other large plants opened, Lynchburg changed from being a "mill town," and Amherst became increasingly a "bedroom community" for broader work venues. There had previously been Amherst residents who actually *bicycled* to the American Cyanamid location.

The downsizing of this kind of large-scale industrial production did not change the fact that Amherst was more and more peripheral to employment locales. Although other business and industry moved into the area in the 1970s, such as the Southeastern Headquarters of the Continental Telephone Company, inevitable changes occurred over the years with mergers and relocations. Society in general became much more mobile, with frequent job transfers to other cities and states becoming the norm for many people.

The Zane G. Snead Industrial Park located off the Boxwood Farm Road did much to help keep jobs in Amherst. Named after the banker and former chairman of the Amherst Industrial Development Authority, the park was built in 1970 and attracted Hermle Black Forest Clock, a German corporation that manufactured clock movements, as its first tenant in 1977. Continental Telephone operated a training facility in the park and Buffalo Air Handling constructed a plant there to manufacture large air handling equipment. As of 2010, the clock firm discontinued manufacturing products at its location in the park.

In 1992, First Brands Corporation, now a unit of Clorox, opened a plant in the industrial park for the manufacture of plastic products such as Glad bags.

Although not located near the town, Virginia Fibre (now Greif Brothers) began operating its paper mill on the James River near Gladstone during the early 1970s. The firm has had a significant impact on the town and county economy over the years.

Construction began on a second industrial park in 2000 east of town off Route 60. The L. Barnes Brockman Sr. Business and Industrial Park would become home to Fairmont Crossing, a Centra Health extended-care facility, and Mutual Telecom Services. Brockman was a long-time businessman in the town and county and, like Snead, a former chairman of the town's Industrial Development Authority.

Combined with county and school employees and nearby Sweet Briar College, firms in the two industrial parks gave the town a diverse employment base.

Over the years, transportation became more universally available. One elderly resident, when asked why Amherst never sustained a community movie theatre, said off-handedly, "Most people enjoyed going to Lynchburg to see a show." A trip to Lynchburg was no longer an event to be planned as a special occasion—people began to "jump into the car and run into Lynchburg," sometimes more than once in a day's time. Shopping, dining out, entertainment—all became more far-flung with mobility. By the 1960s, teenage "cruising" (or just "roamin' around") was spreading the circle of activity beyond the town, and downtown Amherst of old was gradually becoming a thing of the past.

Educational opportunities broadened, first with county-wide consolidation of the high school and gradual elimination of the "neighborhood school." Until mid-century, high school graduation was the ultimate academic goal for many small-town youngsters. Many passed up even that milestone because agricultural interests and other local employers' needs did not require it. With greater prosperity, World War II's "GI Bill," and expanding opportunities, more and more Amherst youth left for college. If they returned to the area (and many did not), their requirements for a satisfactory lifestyle were often greater than what could be provided locally.

The combination of a county high school and the greater availability of cars introduced students to new people and broader horizons. Amherst teens usually headed to Madison Heights, perceived by many to be "where the action is." Discrete separations between communities along Route 29 became blurred, with businesses encroaching into the residential corridor.

Changing roles of women in society meant that girls graduated from high school with their sights set toward goals significantly different from those of their female counterparts of the first half-century. Educational opportunities abounded, with careers often demanding moves to larger metropolitan areas.

Television and the expanded media began the continuing evolutionary process of homogenizing Americans. Becoming a universal presence, television brought the world into the American home, and now technological adjuncts and successors are myriad—fax, email, Internet, texting, and beyond. From the social perspective, impromptu parties and small backyard get-togethers among family members and neighbors, as well as Sunday afternoons with grandparents, aunts, uncles, and cousins, many of whom now may live hundreds of miles away, are diminishing in frequency. Such gatherings were once the staple of Amherst social life.

The traffic circle fountain stands frozen in time in the winter of 2007.
Town of Amherst photo

The generalized Americanese one hears on television has gone far to eliminate the distinctive drawl and Scots-Irish vowel ("ou," as in "out") once characteristic of Amherst and Central Virginia speech. Events once remote from everyday concerns now become large and pervasive (even *invasive*)—from the trivial (Tiny Tim and his wedding, the "new Coke," the Balloon Boy) to the sensational (OJ Simpson, Princess Diana) to the socially important (Vietnam, the turbulent economy, terrorism, Iraq and Afghanistan).

Implicit in all these factors has been the change in race relations. Prior to the 1960s, virtually every component of Amherst society was racially segregated—with the revolution in civil rights fostering more favorable circumstances for all in jobs, travel and relocation, and more meaningful education. The biggest racial divide today, perhaps, is geographical, with the white cemetery on the north end of town and the black cemetery on the south end.

And so . . . The '70s, '80s, '90s and the first decade of the 21st century, maybe a time best characterized as engulfing the area in "greater suburbia," have brought the town of Amherst to the beginning of its second hundred years. One can still hang out at the coffee shop—again called Travelers—but also have his pick of dining venues from Amherst to Lynchburg and even beyond, with selections representing the offerings of several continents; work in businesses or industries with international connections; hear other languages spoken among patrons in stores and businesses; go to Broadway shows on tour, or major college and professional cultural and athletic events, all within a day's roundtrip, rather than just wait for the circus to show up.

And . . . who's to say what is the best of all possible worlds—then or now? ∞

Paul Wailes III, in carriage driven by Cy Giles, leads as parade marshal for the Amherst Centennial parade, June 12, 2010
Lee Luther Jr. photo

WHAT DOES THE FUTURE HOLD?

By Jack Hobbs

For more than 100 years, the government of the Town of Amherst has:

- Worked to keep the town's residents safe and to keep our community free from crime.

- Produced and delivered clean water to the houses and businesses in the community.

- Removed pollution from the water leaving our buildings before it goes back "to the creek."

- Planned for orderly and appropriate growth via land use regulation and capital improvement programs.

- Collected, kept track of, and disbursed many millions of dollars in tax and utility fee revenues.

- And expected hard work and responsibility from those who are elected, appointed to committees, hired as consultants or contractors, or employed by the town.

It seems that every small town has a theme that matches these words at the bottom of the town's stationery: "Respecting the past. Attending the present. Concentrating on the future." This is a good vision for the future of the town since we need to learn from the past—including the projects and programs that went well and those that failed—so we can act now to build a better community. As former Town Manager Rufus Scott has said, "We're all just temporary occupants and merely building on the foundations constructed by those that came before us, as those that will follow will build on ours." This is our challenge and our responsibility.

Life was radically different before the town incorporated in 1910. Amherst Courthouse was a happening place back then during court and market days. It was certainly a rough and tumble environment, with numerous saloons and horse racing and fist fights on Main Street being almost normal activities. Such conveniences as automobiles, telephones, and electricity had been invented, but they were not available in Amherst.

Other amenities our community did not have were municipal water and sewers, refuse collection, zoning and building codes, paved roads, a library or a fire department. Some elements of life that have come and gone since the town's incorporation include big satellite dishes and video stores, parking meters, orange VDOT trucks, purely local banks, and the effort to put a man on the moon.

Although today we're in a time of extreme change and it feels like—at least on a national level—decline, all is not lost. The folks in Amherst are an optimistic and resourceful bunch. Amherst has a solid and diverse economy as a result of Sweet Briar College, the good employers in our industrial parks, and our timber and courthouse industries. We didn't boom over the past couple of decades like a lot of places did, but—and with no disrespect to a lot of our neighbors who are currently without jobs—as a community we didn't exactly go bust when those other places did either.

What does our future look like? Planners are known to have a tendency to overestimate what will happen in the next three years but underestimate what will happen in the next twenty. Whether anyone is qualified to predict what our community will look like several decades from now is questionable. On the other hand, it is an interesting exercise to take a quick look at three areas that might undergo significant change:

Physical development

It might take twenty years, but there will come a day when we will not recognize the area along South Main Street south of the high school. This will be driven by traffic patterns that have changed as a result of the configuration of the new bypass. In addition to commercial buildings and perhaps some residential development, we might even have a new grocery store in that area some day.

Amherst is like a lot of other places in America that have aging infrastructure. We have about sixty miles of town-owned water and sewer pipe, and unless we replace about a mile per year we are falling behind—and we are falling behind. This could mean costly and tremendously inconvenient breaks and sewer stoppages for the town. Rate-paying customers could suffer from service interruptions or even property damage from flooding. And this does not count the fact that other parts of the water and sewer system, such as the plants, pump stations and tanks, are continuing to age. Properly maintaining them will be increasingly costly in the coming years.

Economics

Most folks agree that Amherst is on the verge of being "discovered." Because of our diversity, industrial parks, solid infrastructure and excellent work ethic, Amherst does have good prospects for growth and economic revival after the economy recovers and America gets its swagger back. The downside is that it looks like it will be several years before this will come to pass.

People want good, or even more, municipal services but are less willing to pay for them. Over the past few decades we have seen the consolidation of sewage treatment, health care, jails and airports. In the future we will probably see more of this "regionalism" in areas such as water and sewer utilities, road maintenance and schools. This is not to suggest that this is either

148

good or bad, but it is definitely a trend that is fed by the desire to deliver services in the most efficient way through economies of scale.

Social and cultural

It appears that we are moving away from our faith in institutions. These include:

- Our churches, which have shown a decline in membership and general participation over the past few decades.

- Public education has been tarnished somewhat, perhaps because our county schools are taken for granted and teaching is not the honored profession it once was.

- Instead of being viewed as public service providers, we now refer to the town and county as "governments." And for some reason that word has a negative connotation these days.

- Finally, there is a lower priority on being good neighbors and having good neighbors these days than there was just a few years back. Good neighbors have been, and will continue to be, a hallmark of life in Amherst.

So what do we do? A local leader commented during one of the Centennial Celebration events that the reason Amherst has been so successful is that it is a community first and a town second. In summary, the town corporation is only a vehicle used to accomplish community goals such as maintaining law and order and providing utility services. An incorporated town is just an organizational mechanism.

What is important is the community. Being good neighbors has carried this community for the last 100 years, and it is clear that continuing that tradition will serve us well in the years to come.

We need to keep working to improve our community and, most certainly, to leave it better than it was when we found it. ෨

Jack Hobbs is Amherst's Town Manager.

The authors' entry in the 2010 Centennial Parade, a 1955 Pontiac Star Chief.
Anne Hanger photo

Appendix

View looking north on Main Street, photographed at the same time as the cover picture. Trucks at left belong to Wade Wood (half of truck is visible) and Will Kent, both grocers.
Amherst County Historical Museum photo

151

View from Depot Street toward Second Street.
Paul Wailes III photo

TIMELINE OF AMHERST

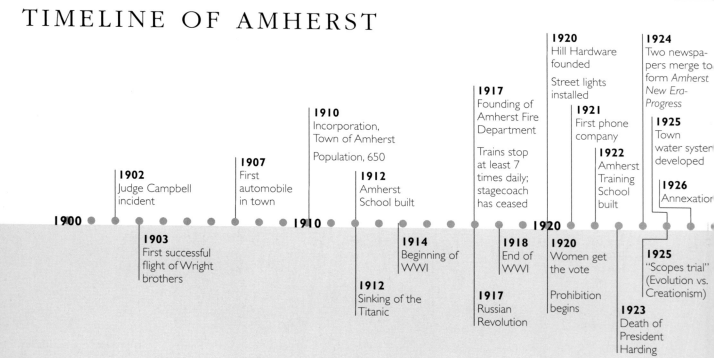

1920
Hill Hardware founded

Street lights installed

1924
Two newspapers merge to form *Amherst New Era-Progress*

1917
Founding of Amherst Fire Department

Trains stop at least 7 times daily; stagecoach has ceased

1921
First phone company

1925
Town water system developed

1910
Incorporation, Town of Amherst

Population, 650

1922
Amherst Training School built

1926
Annexation

1907
First automobile in town

1912
Amherst School built

1902
Judge Campbell incident

1900

1910

1920

1903
First successful flight of Wright brothers

1914
Beginning of WWI

1918
End of WWI

1920
Women get the vote

Prohibition begins

1925
"Scopes trial" (Evolution vs. Creationism)

1912
Sinking of the Titanic

1917
Russian Revolution

1923
Death of President Harding

William Yancey, center, had a blacksmith shop on West Court Street. His mother was "Sis" Yancey, the local midwife.
Marianna Penn photo

1930
Sunnyside
Boxwood Farm
begins operation

1931
Road
through
Amherst
paved

1935
Bigby Davis begins
33-year tenure as
town clerk

1936
Amherst traffic
circle installed

Thomas Hughes'
gas station
and restaurant
opened

De-annexation

1947
Caution light
installed at
Second and
Main Streets

1950
Parking
meters
installed

1953
New
Drummond's
store opens

1956
Closing of
town schools;
countywide
consolida-
tion of high
schools

1959
Founding of
Amherst Life
Saving Crew

930 • • • • • • • • • • • • • 1940 • • • • • • • • • • • 1950 • • • • • • • • • •

1927
Lindbergh crosses
the Atlantic

1929
Wall Street crash

Beginning of Great
Depression

1933
FDR takes
office
Prohibition
ends

1936
FDR
re-
elected

1938
Orson Welles "Martian broadcast"

1939
WWII begins in Europe
"Gone with the Wind"

1940
FDR elected to
3rd term

1941
Attack on
Pearl Harbor
USA enters
war

1944
D-Day: Allied
landings in
Normandy,

1945
Death of FDR

End of WWII

1948
"Dewey Defeats
Truman"

Birth of Israel

1950
War
erupts in
Korea

1952
Eisenhower
elected
President

1953
Armistice ends
Korean War

1956
Ike re-elected, Suez
crisis, uprising in
Hungary

1957
Sputnik

153

Rob Mantiply and Gordon Proffitt, foreground, and Jim Pendleton, meat cutter, in the background, in Mantiply's Store, around 1938.
Robbie Howell photo

Jim Warwick, a talented plumber who served the needs of the townspeople for several decades, kept his tools in Bill Yancey's blacksmith shop.
Jean Higginbotham photo

1970
New Amherst Elementary School opens

Zane Snead Industrial Park opens

1969
Water tower erected on Waugh's Ferry Road

1971
Amherst bypass opens

1974
Willard Douglas appointed judge of Richmond Juvenile & Domestic Relations Court

1988
L.F. Payne, Jr., elected to U.S. Congress

1968
New fire station opens

Amherst population 1200

1972
Dorothy Dickey, first woman elected to town council

1987
New Amherst Life Saving Crew headquarters built

1960

1970

1980

1960
JFK elected president

1963
JFK assassinated

1969
U.S. landing on the moon

1979
Gas price crisis

Iranian militants take over U.S. embassy

1986
Challenger shuttle disaster

1962
Cuban missile crisis

1968
Assassinations of M.L. King, R.F. Kennedy. Nixon elected president

1974
Nixon resigns presidency

1988
George H.W. Bush wins presidency

1967
"Six Day War" in Middle East

1973
Cease fire ends U.S. role in Vietnam

1976
U.S. Bicentennial

Carter elected president

1981
U.S. hostages freed in Iran

Assassination attempts on Reagan, Pope John Paul II

1965
U.S. involvement in Vietnam becomes general

1972
Nixon re-elected. Watergate scandal erupts

1975
Communists take over Vietnam

Patty Hearst case consumes public

1980
Reagan wins presidency

154

View from Second Street
toward Main Street, in the 1920s.
Paul Wailes III photo

1991
Eddie Rodwell
elected first
black mayor

1992
Police chief Haney Mottley
retires after 39 years of service

1993
Annexation

1995
Stop light installed

2000
Vance Wilkins elected
Speaker of the House
of Delegates

Opening of Barnes
Brockman Sr.
Business Park

Amherst census
2251

2005
Water treatment
plant upgraded

2006
Fountain
installed in
traffic circle

2009
Elimination of pay
parking meters;
unveiling of "Art
Meters"

New water
tank installed on
Union Hill Road

2000

2010

1991
Collapse
of U.S.S.R.

1996
Clinton
re-elected

1998
Clinton
impeached

2005
Hurricane
Katrina
devastates
New
Orleans

2010
U.S. role in Iraq ends, troops assigned to
combat in Afghanistan

Health care, other adjustments underway

2009
Bank and business collapse deepens

2003
U.S. allies invade,
occupy Iraq

2008
Election of Barrack Obama, first non-Caucasian U.S.
president

2001
"9-11" terrorist attacks—
nearly 3,000 killed

2007
Recession begins with
increasing business
failure

2000
Disputed presidential election
ends in George W. Bush victory

155

Index